behavior and accomplishments over time and situations, and these data can be used as criterion validity measures for I/O Psychology practices. In a complementary fashion, I/O Psychology provides measures of employee perceptions, and these provide useful social validity data for behavior analysis and OBM practices. They admonish both fields in a constructive manner, and their synergistic approach provides a blueprint for maximizing organizational effectiveness.

Luthans, Youssef, and Rawski continue to innovate with the concepts and practices of Psychological Capital and reinforcing feedback. They present results relevant to problem solving, mastery orientation, and innovation from a large sample of working adults. The theoretical differences between the OBM and I/O Psychology fields can become blurred, but in a good way, when this type of integrated research is conducted. Their integration furthers both research and managerial practices that foster positive change in organizations, and it is promising as one model for possible future OBM-I/O work.

Employee engagement is a relatively new topic in I/O Psychology that, like many other variables, arose from and is promoted in consulting work. Ludwig and Frazier provide a nice analysis of it from an OBM perspective. Engagement is related to both management practices and important outcomes, but it may be too ambiguous a concept for usefulness in OBM. One could argue that it needs to be objectively and behaviorally defined, but the behaviors that would represent it may already be known in both OBM and I/O Psychology. It is probably well-represented in OBM by an environment with wide availability of positive reinforcement and in I/O Psychology by a blend of variables such as organizational citizenship behaviors, work involvement, and organizational commitment. Overall, psychological constructs such as engagement are often measured in I/O Psychology (usually through surveys) without providing a clear direction for practical improvement; OBM can be used, however, to provide ready and operational action.

We want to thank all of the authors for their excellent contributions to this edited book. The interactions we had with all of them were pleasurable, intellectually stimulating, and we hope, useful to both fields. We gained more from their work than they likely know. They performed well, and we greatly appreciate their contributions to this project. We wish to thank Tim Ludwig for suggesting this project as a special issue of the *Journal Organizational Behavior Management* at the OBM Network meeting of the Association for Behavior Analysis: International conference in Phoenix in 2009. He has been extremely supportive, and we are indebted to him for his encouragement, help, and generosity these past three years. Finally, as Co-Editors we are donating all royalties from this project to the Chris Anderson Research Grant Applications for graduate students in the OBM Network (CMJ) and the Industrial/Organizational Psychology Association (IOPA) for graduate students in Industrial and Organizational Psychology at Central Michigan University (TAB).

References

Beehr, T. A., Jex, S. M., & Ghosh, P. (2001). The management of occupational stress. In C. M. Johnson, W. K. Redmon, & T. C. Mawhinney (Eds.), *Handbook of organizational performance: Behavior analysis and management*, (pp. 228-254). New York: Haworth.

Bucklin, B. R., Alvero, A. M., Dickinson, A. M., Austin, J., & Jackson, A. K. (2000). Industrial-Organizational Psychology and Organizational Behavior Management. *Journal of Organizational Behavior Management, 20*(2), 27-75.

Geller, E. S. (2003). Organizational Behavior Management and Industrial/Organizational Psychology. *Journal of Organizational Behavior Management, 22*(2), 111-130.

Handlin, H. C. (1992). The company built upon the golden rule: Lincoln Electric. *Journal of Organizational Behavior Management, 12,* 151-162.

Johnson, C. M., Redmon, W. K, & Mawhinney, T. C. (Eds.)(2001). *Handbook of organizational performance: Behavior analysis and management*. New York: Haworth Press.

O'Hara, K., Johnson, C. M., & Beehr, T. A. (1985). Organizational behavior management in the private sector: A review of empirical research and recommendations for further investigation. *Academy of Management Review, 40,* 848-864.

Integrating Organizational Behavior Management with Industrial and Organizational Psychology

This book examines the intersection of Organizational Behavior Management (OBM) and Industrial and Organizational Psychology (I/O Psychology). It argues that, whilst OBM and I/O Psychology have developed simultaneously, they have done so with minimal integration. I/O Psychology, a somewhat older field, has evolved to become widely accepted, both influencing management and social sciences and being affected by them. It can be viewed as a research-oriented subject that is closely aligned with human resources functions. With regards to the intersection of I/O Psychology with OBM, some practices are more closely related than others; and of those that are related, some are relatively consistent with OBM practices, while others are very inconsistent. Most I/O Psychology interventions focus on many people simultaneously, seeking to ensure that one intervention affects multiple employees as a cost-efficient way to improve organizations, while OBM is usually better than I/O Psychology at improving the behaviors of individuals and smaller groups or workers.

This book provides a framework for understanding differences and similarities between I/O Psychology and OBM, and as such is an innovative compendium for students, scholars, applied psychologists, and human resource specialists. It was originally published as a special issue of the *Journal of Organizational Behavior Management*.

C. Merle Johnson is Professor of Psychology at Central Michigan University, USA. He serves on the editorial board for the *Journal of Organizational Behavior Management*. His research concerns organizational behaviour management, treatment of sleep disorders in children, behavioural pediatrics, and the assessment and treatment of children who have low-incidence disabilities.

Terry A. Beehr is Professor and Director of the Ph.D. Program in I/O Psychology at Central Michigan University, USA. He currently serves as an associate editor on three journals and is on the editorial boards of four more. His research emphases include stress, retirement, career development, leadership, and motivation in organizations.

Integrating Organizational Behavior Management with Industrial and Organizational Psychology

Edited by
C. Merle Johnson and Terry A. Beehr

LONDON AND NEW YORK

First published 2013
by Routledge
2 Park Square, Milton Park, Abingdon, Oxon, OX14 4RN

Simultaneously published in the USA and Canada
by Routledge
711 Third Avenue, New York, NY 10017

Routledge is an imprint of the Taylor & Francis Group, an informa business

© 2013 Taylor & Francis

This book is a reproduction of the *Journal of Organizational Behavior Management*, volume 31, issue 4, with the exception of Chapter 9, which was first published in volume 32, issue 1. The Publisher requests to those authors who may be citing this book to state, also, the bibliographical details of the special issue on which the book was based.

All rights reserved. No part of this book may be reprinted or reproduced or utilised in any form or by any electronic, mechanical, or other means, now known or hereafter invented, including photocopying and recording, or in any information storage or retrieval system, without permission in writing from the publishers.

Trademark notice: Product or corporate names may be trademarks or registered trademarks, and are used only for identification and explanation without intent to infringe.

British Library Cataloguing in Publication Data
A catalogue record for this book is available from the British Library

ISBN13: 978-0-415-62302-5

Typeset in Garamond
by Taylor & Francis Books

Publisher's Note
The publisher would like to make readers aware that the chapters in this book may be referred to as articles as they are identical to the articles published in the special issue. The publisher accepts responsibility for any inconsistencies that may have arisen in the course of preparing this volume for print.

Printed and bound in the United States of America by Publishers Graphics, LLC on sustainably sourced paper.

Library
University of Texas
at San Antonio

Contents

Citation Information   vii

1. Industrial and Organizational Psychology Encounters Organizational Behavior Management: Would You Care to Dance?
   C. Merle Johnson and Terry A. Beehr   1

2. Performance-Based Rewards and Work Stress
   Daniel C. Ganster, Christa E. Kiersch, Rachel E. Marsh, and Angela Bowen   5

3. Promoting Critical Operant-Based Leadership While Decreasing Ubiquitous Directives and Exhortations
   Judith L. Komaki, Michelle L. R. Minnich, Angela R. Grotto, Bret Weinshank, and Michael J. Kern   20

4. Managing Performance to Change Behavior
   Angelo S. DeNisi   46

5. Square Pegs and Round Holes: Ruminations on the Relationship Between Performance Appraisal and Performance Management
   Nicole E. Gravina and Brian P. Siers   61

6. Job Satisfaction: I/O Psychology and Organizational Behavior Management Perspectives
   Thomas C. Mawhinney   72

7. From Job Analysis to Performance Management: A Synergistic Rapprochement to Organizational Effectiveness
   Charles R. Crowell, Donald A. Hantula, and Kari L. McArthur   100

8. A Tale of Two Paradigms: The Impact of Psychological Capital and Reinforcing Feedback on Problem Solving and Innovation
   Fred Luthans, Carolyn M. Youssef, and Shannon L. Rawski   117

9. Employee Engagement and Organizational Behavior Management
   Timothy D. Ludwig and Christopher B. Frazier   135

Index   143

Citation Information

The following chapters were originally published in the *Journal of Organizational Behavior Management*. When citing this material, please use the original issue information and page numbering for each article, as follows:

Chapter 2
Performance-Based Rewards and Work Stress
Daniel C. Ganster, Christa E. Kiersch, Rachel E. Marsh, and Angela Bowen
Journal of Organizational Behavior Management, volume 31, issue 4 (2011) pp. 221-235

Chapter 3
Promoting Critical Operant-Based Leadership While Decreasing Ubiquitous Directives and Exhortations
Judith L. Komaki, Michelle L. R. Minnich, Angela R. Grotto, Bret Weinshank, and Michael J. Kern
Journal of Organizational Behavior Management, volume 31, issue 4 (2011) pp. 236-261

Chapter 4
Managing Performance to Change Behavior
Angelo S. DeNisi
Journal of Organizational Behavior Management, volume 31, issue 4 (2011) pp. 262-276

Chapter 5
Square Pegs and Round Holes: Ruminations on the Relationship Between Performance Appraisal and Performance Management
Nicole E. Gravina and Brian P. Siers
Journal of Organizational Behavior Management, volume 31, issue 4 (2011) pp. 277-287

Chapter 6
Job Satisfaction: I/O Psychology and Organizational Behavior Management Perspectives
Thomas C. Mawhinney
Journal of Organizational Behavior Management, volume 31, issue 4 (2011) pp. 288-315

Chapter 7
From Job Analysis to Performance Management: A Synergistic Rapprochement to Organizational Effectiveness
Charles R. Crowell, Donald A. Hantula, and Kari L. McArthur
Journal of Organizational Behavior Management, volume 31, issue 4 (2011) pp. 316-332

Chapter 8
A Tale of Two Paradigms: The Impact of Psychological Capital and Reinforcing Feedback on Problem Solving and Innovation
Fred Luthans, Carolyn M. Youssef, and Shannon L. Rawski
Journal of Organizational Behavior Management, volume 31, issue 4 (2011) pp. 333-350

Chapter 9
Employee Engagement and Organizational Behavior Management
Timothy D. Ludwig and Christopher B. Frazier
Journal of Organizational Behavior Management, volume 32, issue 1 (2012) pp. 75-82

Industrial and Organizational Psychology Encounters Organizational Behavior Management: Would You Care to Dance?

C. Merle Johnson and Terry A. Beehr
Central Michigan University

With a former graduate student, we published a review 25 years ago concerning organizational behavior management (OBM) in the private sector when OBM was a new field (O'Hara, Johnson, & Beehr, 1985). Ten years ago we collaborated again to show how OBM had progressed (Beehr, Jex, & Ghosh, 2001; Johnson, Redmon, & Mawhinney, 2001). As an OBM researcher and an Industrial and Organizational Psychology (I/O Psychology) researcher, we continue to observe the evolution of this field and are fortunate to be able to participate in its development.

Simultaneously I/O Psychology, a somewhat older field, has evolved to become ever more widely accepted, influencing management and social sciences, and being influenced by them. I/O Psychology can be viewed as a research-oriented field in which the findings determine and evaluate many practices related broadly to the human side of organizations. The topics of these findings vary a great deal. They include for example: recommendations for selecting people based on matching their traits with job demands; trying to measure those trait and job environment constructs; motivating employees by making external rewards like pay contingent on performance, or by designing jobs to make internal rewards like pride contingent on performance; finding ways to estimate performance when no clear and objective way to observe it is apparent; figuring out and training leaders how to get subordinates to comply with organizationally preferred behaviors, getting members of workgroups to work well together; finding ways to make employees satisfied as well as productive, and reducing psychological stress in the workplace.

Regarding the intersection of I/O Psychology with OBM, some practices of I/O Psychology are more closely related to OBM practices than others. Of those that are related, some practices are relatively consistent with OBM, whilst others are very inconsistent. Furthermore, on average, most I/O Psychology interventions focus on many people at once—often seeking to make one intervention that will make large numbers of people happier and more productive on average—as a cost-efficient way to improve organizations. OBM is usually better than I/O Psychology at improving the behavior of individuals and smaller groups or workers. A final point about I/O Psychology is that some parts of it have a heavy investment in, and belief in, the value of statistics and psychological measurement, some of which are complex; OBM tends to emphasize repeated measures of behavior over time and situations and uses simpler statistics for their direct observations of behavior.

Previous comparisons between the fields were published in the *Journal of Organizational Behavior Management* (JOBM; Bucklin, Alvero, Dickinson, Austin, & Jackson, 2000; Geller, 2003). These classic reviews provided a framework for understanding differences and similarities between I/O Psychology and OBM, and we encourage readers who are not already familiar with these articles to examine them.

We will avoid labeling the contributors to this special issue as being either OBM or I/O professionals, but we subjectively judge that about half of the authors have a mostly I/O orientation and explain OBM-relevant issues from their perceptions. The other half have mostly an OBM orientation and explain I/O-relevant issues from their perspective. We judge that each knows something about the other field, but the depth of this cross-knowledge varies. This makes provocative reading for someone interested in the relationship between OBM and I/O Psychology.

In the opening chapter Ganster, Kiersch, Marsh, and Bowen provide a stimulating depiction of the interplay between pay-for-performance and work stress. They acknowledge that productivity is enhanced with variable pay systems that are contingent upon productivity, but wonder whether such pay systems increase work stress and potential health problems. Well-controlled research on this relationship is wanting. Long-term pay-for-performance companies such as Lincoln Electric (Handlin, 1992) would be the type of organizational system in which researchers could study physical health-care costs, preferably with comparable controls.

Komaki, Minnich, Grotto, Weinshank, and Kern present data from a managerial training program conducted in both a private and public organizational setting, a program incorporating continued work on the well-developed Operant Model of Effective Supervision. Their in-basket assessment demonstrates that seasoned managers can learn to monitor employee performance and then apply effective consequences to maintain the employee's newly acquired behaviors. These field studies demonstrate better managerial efficacy than the more commonly used strategies involving only antecedent stimuli such as giving directions and orders.

DeNisi documents the evolution of performance appraisal and how performance management is a broader and more useful approach. Interesting theoretical and organizational questions arise in his chapter, and he succinctly explains why performance management is so useful for enhancing employee development and organizational effectiveness. The chapter by Gravina and Siers follows; their integrative approach illustrates how to blend OBM with I/O Psychology. They elucidate many of the points DeNisi presents, and they advocate that each field would benefit from drawing from the other–a position we share as guest editors for this book.

Mawhinney presents a scholarly history of job satisfaction, starting with a contribution by Thorndike from the first volume of *Journal of Applied Psychology* in 1917. He notes the developments from classic tomes, differences and similarities in the two fields (including their historical roots), and argues well that measures such as job satisfaction could provide social validity for OBM projects, as well as encouraging organizational social responsibility. I/O Psychology has increasingly embraced theory, whilst OBM has been less theory driven; Mawhinney presents the controversial issue regarding whether OBM should promote an integrated collection of its work as a theory, which raises the issue of what a theory is.

In their chapter, Crowell, Hantula, and McArthur blend personnel psychology and OBM in a service organization. Their excellent work echoes Mawhinney's position and our own viewpoint: OBM provides viable objective direct measures of employee

Performance-Based Rewards and Work Stress

DANIEL C. GANSTER, CHRISTA E. KIERSCH, RACHEL E. MARSH,
and ANGELA BOWEN

Colorado State University, Fort Collins, Colorado, USA

Even though reward systems play a central role in the management of organizations, their impact on stress and the well-being of workers is not well understood. We review the literature linking performance-based reward systems to various indicators of employee stress and well-being. Well-controlled experiments in field settings suggest that certain types of performance-based reward systems, such as piece rate pay, cause increases in psychological and physiological stress. Such findings are mirrored in nonexperimental studies as well, but the causal mechanisms for such effects are not well understood. We argue that reward systems generally deserve much more attention in the work stress literature, and identify several mediating and moderating variables worthy of study.

Workplace stress is believed to be a major contributor to both mental and physical health problems. According to surveys of workers across many occupations, work demands comprise the most stressful experiences in the lives of about 25% of workers and are implicated in a wide range of health complaints such as cardiovascular disease, depression, and musculoskeletal disorders (NIOSH, 1999). The last several decades have witnessed the development of a mature research literature investigating the causes and consequences of work stress that incorporates many different disciplines. In addition to thousands of journal articles, several handbooks (e.g., Quick & Tetrick, 2011) and annual series (Perrewé & Ganster, 2010) are devoted to summarizing and integrating this large body of research. Many specific aspects of the workplace have been studied as potential causes of mental and physical health problems. In this article, we will examine the evidence concerning one important work characteristic—performance-based rewards—that, although they play a central role in performance management systems, have received far less attention than many other potential stressors regarding their role in work stress.

We focus on performance-contingent pay because it is a major approach to compensation in most countries around the world. Performance-contingent pay is a type of variable pay system, and variable pay systems range from those that include a stable base level of pay that is supplemented with performance-based pay (e.g., bonuses, commissions, profit sharing) to those that base the worker's entire compensation on their performance (e.g., sales commissions and piece rate pay plans). Variable pay plans can also vary in the extent to which they are based on company-wide performance indicators, on team performance, or individual performance. There is ample theoretical justification for the use of performance-based pay schemes in the organizational literature in terms of their expected effects on job performance. Expectancy theory and equity theory, as well as the operant model, all provide explanations for why performance-based pay should create incentives for higher performance (Lawler, 1990). The theoretical counter-point has mainly come from intrinsic motivation theorists (Deci, 1975). Their argument rests on the assumption that individuals attribute a locus of causality to their own behaviors, which can range from internal to external. From this perspective, performance-linked rewards will lead to the formation of an extrinsic locus of causality, and the subsequent extrinsic motivation detracts from one's intrinsic motivation to engage in the activity. Eventually, this reduction in intrinsic motivation is hypothesized to lead to reduced performance on the task. In later years this theoretical perspective was broadened to incorporate well-being outcomes as well as task motivation (Ryan & Deci, 2000). A meta-analysis of the relationship between financial incentives and work performance, however, reveals a significant and robust relationship (Jenkins, Mitra, Gupta, & Shaw, 1998). Jenkins et al. (1998) found an average corrected effect size of .34 between performance-based pay and quantitative measures of performance, but a nonsignificant one for performance quality. The quantitative performance relationship was weakest in laboratory experiments (.24), followed by field experiments (.48), and strongest in experimental simulations (.56). These relationships did not differ across tasks classified as intrinsic versus extrinsic.

Reward plans as actually implemented in work organizations are complex, and their impact on different indicators of performance can vary widely depending on how they are designed and administered. But there is sufficiently compelling theoretical and empirical rationale for their use to make them ubiquitous in almost every industrialized country. Even in some European countries, in which some forms of performance-based pay plans are seen as controversial, they are still commonly employed. For example, in a sample of 90 large German firms, 63 reported using a performance-related pay plan, and about half of these had only recently introduced or extended such plans (Kurdelbusch, 2002). Thus, performance-based rewards are commonplace throughout work organizations worldwide. If they constitute a significant source of stress that adversely affects the well-being of workers, this would have large implications for designing healthy workplaces. In comparison to the body of empirical research investigating performance and productivity-related outcomes of performance-based reward plans, empirical studies of employee health and well-being outcomes are relatively scarce.

WHY MIGHT PERFORMANCE-BASED REWARDS BE STRESSFUL?

According to the transactional model of stress (Folkman & Lazarus, 1990), the level of stress experienced by an individual is determined by how that person cognitively appraises the events encountered. Upon exposure to some working condition or event, individuals' primary appraisals assess whether the condition represents a threat to well-being or a benign or challenging condition. If the primary appraisal is one of threat, a secondary appraisal generates the individuals' estimates of their ability to effectively cope with it. Performance-based reward systems very likely trigger such cognitive appraisals. As Brief and Atieh (1987) stressed more than twenty years ago, economic outcomes are likely to be among the most salient potential stressors encountered in the workplace. The stressful effects of job loss and employment insecurity have been well-known for a long time (Kahn, 1981). Short of actual loss of one's job, however, is the issue of income security and predictability. Because a performance-based reward system renders at least a part of the worker's compensation as variable, it is likely to be seen as a significant feature of the work environment that will trigger a stress-related cognitive appraisal process.

The critical question concerns whether individuals will appraise such systems as threats or challenges. On the one hand, a performance-based reward system could be appraised as a challenge or opportunity if individuals believed that they could determine the level of performance that was linked to their pay. Organizational behavior management (OBM) principles, for example, require reinforcement to be contingent on behavior that individuals can control (Duncan & Smoot, 2001; Frisch & Dickinson, 1990). In expectancy theory terms, this would refer to their effort-to-performance expectancy, which could be determined by a variety of factors, including the nature of the tasks themselves in terms of their controllability or aspects of the individuals such as their self-efficacy. On the other hand, individuals might perceive little direct control over the performance metrics that determine their pay. Uncertainty and lack of control over important outcomes have been shown to be among the most important correlates of mental and physical well being in the workplace (Kain & Jex, 2010). Thus, the concept of control is likely to be an important factor in determining the impact of performance-based reward systems on well-being. Intuitively, it would seem that the closer rewards are linked to the performance of individual workers, the more likely that they will perceive that they have control over the rewards. It follows that there will be less perceived individual control when rewards are based on team, departmental, or organization-wide performance metrics. Such control beliefs may not follow the use of performance-based pay plans, however, if the performance metrics are seen by workers as biased, arbitrary, or based on favoritism, as is often the case when performance is assessed with subjective appraisals.

In addition to control perceptions, moreover, performance-based rewards can indirectly generate other working conditions that can have a pernicious effect on worker well-being. For example, whereas rewards that are tightly linked to individual performance have the potential to augment workers' sense of control over their pay, such reward systems might also be accompanied by intrusive performance monitoring systems, cooperation-reducing competition among workers, and reductions in coworker support, all of which might negate any beneficial effects of control. Pfeffer and Langton (1993), for example, demonstrated that in academic departments with greater levels of salary dispersion (presumably based on performance-based pay raises), job satisfaction was lower and there was less collaboration among faculty members. Pfeffer (2007) has argued that rewarding workers on the basis of individual performance can create dysfunctional distinctions among workers and perceptions of unfairness. Perhaps for these reasons a number of surveys have indicated widespread dissatisfaction with individual performance-based pay plans (Hewitt and Associates, 2004).

In summary, how individuals are rewarded at work is perhaps one of the most salient features of the work environment and can serve as a source of satisfaction, challenge, and fulfillment, or a source of uncertainty, mistrust, and perceived inequity. Although much research has examined the effects of performance-based pay on performance itself, there has not been a systematic review of its effects on worker stress and well-being. Our objective in this article, then, is to review studies that have examined relationships between performance-based reward systems and various indicators of employee stress and well-being. We have attempted to be broadly inclusive and review any study that compared different reward systems on the basis of affective, behavioral, or physiological responses, except those pertaining to job performance itself. As we note below, this literature varies widely in the research strategies used, and includes both experimental and nonexperimental studies. We conclude with a methodological critique of this literature and suggestions for further research.

REVIEW OF THE EMPIRICAL LITERATURE

We have categorized the available empirical evidence concerning relationships between performance-contingent rewards and employee well-being into two types: experimental studies conducted in the laboratory and field and nonexperimental field studies. Most of the research has fallen under the second category, examining stress and strain outcomes of performance-contingent pay largely using survey research methods. As we explain below, each of these two research strategies has its own strengths and weaknesses, and we conclude our review with an integration of these literatures that accounts for methodological limitations in each.

Experimental Laboratory and Field Studies

Laboratory experiments examining performance-based pay and other rewards mostly stem from an interest in testing intrinsic motivation and self-determination hypotheses derived from cognitive evaluation theory (CET; Deci & Ryan, 1987). The premise of CET is that making a reward contingent on meeting a specific level of performance will have the effect of reducing the worker's sense of autonomy. This hypothesis is relevant to the question of stress and well-being because worker control and autonomy have played such a key role in the work stress literature (Ganster & Fusilier, 1989, Karasek & Theorell, 1990). If performance-based rewards produce decrements in autonomy, this would have significant implications for worker stress and well-being, because autonomy or control is one of the most robust correlates of stress outcomes in the workplace (Kain & Jex, 2010). This hypothesis was tested in a laboratory experiment by Eisenberger, Rhoades, and Cameron (1999), who instructed students to perform a visual comparison task and receive a monetary reward based on meeting a set level of performance. They found that in the contingent reward condition, participants reported higher levels of perceived autonomy while doing the task, which clearly contradicted CET. In a later series of two experiments, however, Houlfort, Koestner, Joussemet, Natel-Vivier, and Lekes (2002) confirmed Eisenberger et al.'s (1999) conclusion that contingent reward did not lead to feelings of social control. But their results also supported the CET prediction that contingent rewards would create feelings of pressure and anxiety. The discrepant findings were reconciled by Houlfort et al.'s (2002) contention that Eisenberger et al.'s measure of control did not differentiate between affective autonomy and decisional autonomy. In other words, contingent rewards might not lead to feelings of a loss of decisional control and may even boost feelings of competence, while at the same time they may increase feelings of pressure and anxiety. Another series of laboratory experiments by Muraven, Rosman, and Gagné (2007), however, uncovered no effects of contingent rewards on mood, arousal, or anxiety.

Thus, laboratory studies do not completely support the CET notion that contingent rewards will lead to feelings of loss of control, at least in terms describing individuals' sense of their own control over their decisions. There is some evidence, however, that working under contingent rewards can be anxiety-producing, although this is not always replicated in different laboratories and with different tasks. Of course, laboratory studies are of very short duration, and the rewards at stake are very minor outcomes in the lives of the individuals participating in them. When one's livelihood and economic security are contingent on meeting performance criteria, however, the anxiety effects sometimes evident in the laboratory might be significantly greater.

Experiments in field settings have generated more compelling evidence than those produced in the laboratory that pay systems can affect stress levels in employees. Among the first quasi-experimental studies was the longitudinal investigation of tax accountants reported by Friedman, Rosenman, and Carroll (1958), who tracked the blood cholesterol levels of tax accountants as they approached the tax deadline and after workloads later returned to normal. They observed that cholesterol levels rose precipitously during tax season and dropped back to normal afterward. Although they did not isolate the specific effects of performance-contingent rewards, it is reasonable to assume that accountants perceive a contingency between their meeting deadlines and their subsequent compensation, especially to the extent that they are billing on a fee for service basis. Levi (1972) was the first to report an experimental examination of piece rate pay on stress outcomes in a natural field setting. He studied 12 female invoicing clerks who performed a few simple operations and produced postal invoices. For four days Levi collected self-report and urinary catecholamine measures of stress, with the participants alternating two days on hourly wage and two days on piece rate. He found that subjective reports of fatigue and physical discomfort, as well as levels of adrenaline and noradrenaline, were significantly higher on piece rate days than on salary days. Production rates also doubled on piece rate days, although Levi concluded that exertion rates were not likely sufficient to account for the differences in stress hormones. Two other field experiments that specifically manipulated performance-based pay were conducted by Timio and colleagues (Timio & Gentili, 1976; Timio, Gentili, & Pede, 1979). We review these in more detail because of the rigor of their designs.

Timio and Gentili (1976) randomly assigned confectioner workers to one of two groups in a cross-over design in which each worker alternated between four-day schedules of working on a piece rate pay system or an hourly wage. One group went from salary to piece rate and back to salary while the other group went from piece rate to salary and then back to piece rate. Groups were compared on daily measures of adrenaline, noradrenaline, and 11-hydroxycorticosteroids, hormones that are elevated under conditions of stress and arousal. The effects of piece rate pay were clearly evident, with rates of stress hormones two to three times higher during piece rate days than during hourly wage days. Timio, Gentili, and Pede (1979) replicated these results with a larger group of confectioner workers using the same alternating schedule that varied on and off piece rate pay. The results for stress hormones were again significantly elevated by working under piece rate pay. In order to test whether workers would adapt to such conditions over time, they replicated the comparisons six months later and found the same results.

These studies are rare in that they involved a high level of experimental control and were conducted under real working conditions. They raise questions, however, about what mechanism produced the dramatic increases in stress hormones under piece rate pay. Were these effects generated by psychological stress responses such as anxiety, felt pressure, or feelings of uncertainty, or do they reflect the effects of increased physical exertion that might be expected when individuals work under an incentive system? Unfortunately, in neither study did the investigators collect self-report measures that might have served as potential mediating variables. Timio et al. (1979), however, collected physical measures of exertion by sampling the amount of oxygen expired by workers under each condition. From these samples they could estimate physical energy expenditures, which did not differ across payment conditions. These data seem to argue against the alternative explanation that increased productive effort accounted for stress hormone elevations. This conclusion also reinforced that made by Levi (1972) that physical exertion effects did not account for differences in stress hormone output observed in his study.

The experimental evidence from laboratory and field studies supports the plausibility of the hypothesis that performance-based pay can induce stress responses that might adversely affect the health of workers. The most compelling evidence comes from the field experiments by Timio and colleagues (Timio & Gentili, 1976; Timio et al., 1979) and Levi (1972) that are able to make a strong case for the causal effects of piece rate payment plans on physiological indicators of stress. Although increased physical exertion does not appear to be the explanatory variables for the effects of piece rate, neither is there direct evidence that the stress hormones were triggered by affective or cognitive stress mediators. We do not know whether the confectioners working on piece rate cognitively appraised their jobs as threatening or high pressure, nor do we know what effects piece rate pay had on their sense of control or self-efficacy. These are important questions for future researchers to address.

Nonexperimental Field Studies

The experimental and quasi-experimental evidence presented thus far suggests a causal effect of performance-based pay on employee well-being, especially pay systems such as piece rate that put all of the workers' pay at risk. We now turn to nonexperimental field investigations of performance-contingent pay. Although nonexperimental studies do not provide strong evidence for causal inferences, such studies in field settings have the capability to examine a wider range of variables that might mediate or moderate the effects of performance-based pay on worker well-being.

One large-scale field study by Brisson, Vinet, Vézina, and Gingras (1989) explored the long-term effects of piecework jobs on severe disability after retirement. In this study, archival information was combined with personal interview data to explore the relationship between number of years working in piecework and prevalence of severe disability after retirement with 533 Quebec female garment workers who had left the garment industry between 1976 and 1985. Results showed that duration of employment in piecework (i.e., jobs in which the worker is paid per garment completed) significantly predicted prevalence of severe disability after retirement —even after accounting for age, smoking, education, task type, and total length of employment. Compared to workers who had been in piecework for 0–4 years, those in piecework for 5–10 years had a risk ratio of 2.2, and those who had been in piecework for 10–19 years had a risk ratio of approximately 3.5. To illustrate the strength of this effect, approximately 25% of women who had been in piecework for 10–19 years had incurred a severe disability, as compared to 9.6% of women who had been in piecework for less than four years (Brisson et al., 1989).

In research that has supported the relationship between performance-based pay and decreased employee well-being, the pay system of interest tends to covary with certain characteristics of the job or work environment. Confounding the effect of payment strategy in Brisson et al.'s study are the stressors inherent in the piecework jobs they examined, including time stress, repetitive motion, and monotony. A study of over 2,500 factory workers in Israel took a closer look at one of these variables, exploring subjective and objective monotony as mediators of the relationship between performance-contingent pay and worker strain (Shirom, Westman, & Melamed, 1999). In this field study, third-party job analysis was used to gather data regarding job characteristics and type of pay system (categorized as time-based, piece rate, individual wage incentives, or group wage incentives), and self-report questionnaires were used to gather data on workers' psychological distress (depression, anxiety, and somatic complaints). After controlling for age, sex, educational attainment, marital status, and ethnic origin, all three performance-based pay systems (piece rate, individual wage incentives, and group wage incentives) were associated with higher levels of self-reported depression and somatic complaints as compared to time-based pay. Piece rate pay also significantly predicted anxiety and had the strongest relationships with all three psychological distress outcomes. Furthermore, both objective (rated by third-party job analysis) and subjective (rated by the worker) monotony partially mediated the relationships between performance-based pay and depression and somatic complaints. This study is informative because it controlled for a series of potentially confounding variables, notably monotony, task cycle time, work underload, and the trait of emotional reactivity. The effect sizes for performance-based pay on the outcome variables, however, were quite small, accounting for only about 1% of the variance in the outcomes.

Two additional job characteristics, heightened workload and lack of job control, have been highlighted as potential mediators in more recent field research. In a large-scale survey study of over 15,000 workers between the ages of 25 and 65 in Taiwan, job characteristics and perceived stress and strain of workers in variable pay systems (including performance-based pay in addition to a fixed salary, piece rate pay with no fixed salary, and time-based pay with no fixed salary) were compared with those of workers in fixed pay systems (workers with fixed salaries only) (Yeh, Cheng, & Chen, 2009). Results of this national survey study showed that employees with performance-based or piece rate pay had higher self-reported personal burnout and work-related burnout than employees with fixed salaries, even after controlling for worker age, education, marital status, employment grade, other job characteristics, and family care workloads. There were distinctions, moreover, among the different forms of variable pay. Workers with performance-based pay added to a fixed salary reported the longest working hours and highest levels of stress, while workers with no fixed salary (with piece rate pay or time-based pay) reported the lowest levels of job control and job satisfaction. In the breadth of this single study, two very different paths from performance-contingent rewards to stress are evident. For workers with performance-based rewards in addition to a fixed salary, heightened time at work covaries with stress and burnout; and for workers with piece rate pay only, low job control and job satisfaction covary with burnout.

Other researchers have supported the direct effect of performance monitoring on worker well-being, indicating that constant and close monitoring may be a potential mediator in the performance-contingent reward and stress relationship. Inherent in this mediation model is the assumption that for pay to be linked with performance, workers' performance must be closely and consistently recorded. In one study of monitoring as a stressor, 745 telecommunication workers working within the same company were compared based upon several psychological and physical health outcomes (Smith, Carayon, Sanders, Lim, & LeGrande, 1992). Employees who were constantly electronically monitored at work perceived their working conditions as significantly more stressful and reported significantly higher levels of psychological tension, anxiety, depression, anger, health complaints, and fatigue (Smith et al., 1992).

The empirical evidence from nonexperimental field studies reviewed thus far suggests that performance-based pay systems are detrimental for employee well-being. However, not all field studies support unconditional negative effects of performance-contingent rewards and pay. In research on organizational leadership, contingent reward leadership style (i.e., leaders who reward subordinates based on performance) has been shown to have a positive relationship with employee well-being. For example, in one study measuring leadership and burnout in a sample of 625 nurses, those who reported having a supervisor high on contingent reward leadership style reported lower levels of emotional exhaustion (one component of burnout) (Stordeur, D'Horre, & Vandenberghe, 2001). Although the effect size was small (with contingent reward leadership accounting for only 2% of the variance in emotional exhaustion), the positive impact of contingent rewards for workers in such a high stress occupation remains noteworthy.

Research on organizational fairness, and specifically on distributive justice, has also suggested a positive relationship between performance-contingent pay and employee well-being. In one example of this research, Howard and Dougherty (2004) collected survey data from 154 employees in ten different companies regarding their companies' payment strategies and their related attitudes. Of all the different payment strategies reported, only that based on personal performance (the "individual output reward strategy") was significantly related to perceptions of high pay fairness (with individual performance-based pay accounting for approximately 9% of the variance in pay fairness perceptions). No other payment strategies (including payment based on group performance, human capital, position in the organization, or market value estimates) had significant positive relationships with either pay satisfaction or pay fairness (Howard & Dougherty, 2004). Although this study did not measure stressors or strain, it did suggest that employees may have some favorable views of or reactions to performance-based pay.

Several potential moderating variables have been proposed that help to explain the inconsistent findings across field studies, including control (or autonomy), performance level, financial requirements, and job type. Building on Karasek's demand-control model (Karasek, 1979), some researchers have argued that performance-contingent rewards will likely cause job demands to increase, but will only lead to employee stress and strain if the employee perceives little job control. In some cases, performance-contingent rewards may be associated with lower perceived control (e.g., employees perceive their supervisor as gaining control instead), and in others they may be associated with higher perceived control (e.g., employees have more control over how much they will earn). In this way, performance-contingent reward systems could be stressful if control is low and could be neutral or even beneficial to employee well-being if control is high. Important questions, therefore, are whether and why employees perceive the same pay system differently and if those perceptions matter for stress reactions.

Researchers have also shown that employees may react differently to performance-contingent rewards depending on their own level of performance. Specifically, employees who perform at lower levels may react more negatively and experience more stress from performance-contingent rewards, while employees who perform at higher levels may react more positively and experience less stress from performance-contingent rewards. In support of this hypothesis, a meta-analysis of the performance and turnover relationship (Williams & Livingstone, 1994) showed that the relationship between performance and turnover is significantly stronger in organizations using a performance-contingent reward system (unweighted rho = −0.27) than in organizations not using a performance-contingent reward system (unweighted rho = −0.18). Presumably, employees with low performance receive less pay and rewards under this system and are thus more likely to be dissatisfied and experience stress. Although turnover is not purely a stress reaction, it might be related to stress reactions. Future research is needed on the potentially complex relationship between an individual's form of pay (piece rate versus others), level of performance, and stress reactions to determine whether higher performers might not be as harmed or might even thrive under an individual performance-based pay system.

Finally, job type has been proposed as an important potential moderator in the performance-contingent rewards and stress relationship (e.g., Howard & Dougherty, 2004). Howard and Dougherty (2004) showed meaningful differences between worker groups in their effort levels and perceptions associated with various pay strategies. However, very little research has examined multiple job types and job levels in the same study, preventing us from making an adequate comparison between white-collar and blue-collar workers, for example. More research is needed to better understand how different job types and levels may change the relationship between performance-contingent rewards and stress.

In sum, the body of nonexperimental field studies investigating the relationship between performance-contingent pay and rewards on employee well-being has yielded mixed results. While the majority of studies have supported the general negative effects of performance-contingent pay, recent research has supported potential moderating and mediating variables and has exposed this issue as less than clear-cut. While these nonexperimental field studies cannot determine causality, they do suggest interesting relationships among variables and provide a snapshot of how employees respond to performance-based pay systems within the complex environments of real organizations.

CONCLUSIONS AND DIRECTIONS FOR FUTURE RESEARCH

Theorists and practitioners have claimed for a long time that performance-based reward systems, and especially piece rate plans, may be injurious to worker health. Yoder (1947) surmised that workers on such systems were likely to overwork themselves to the detriment of their well-being. More recently, Pfeffer (2007) has enumerated the possible unintended consequences of performance-based pay schemes on the social climate of the work group. Despite this long-standing interest, relatively few studies have systematically assessed the stress-related effects of contingent pay. The experimental studies in actual work situations (Levi, 1972; Timio & Gentili, 1976; Timio et al., 1979) provide the most compelling evidence that performance-based pay can generate increased physiological stress responses. But this evidence only comes from piece rate pay and not from other forms of performance-contingent pay. The nonexperimental field studies, while not being able to make a strong case for the causal effects of contingent rewards, suggest that there are psychological and health-related correlates of contingent pay, especially piece rate.

Field research shows that a number of other working conditions tend to covary with performance-contingent pay plans. What some investigators label mediating factors, such as monotony (Shirom et al., 1999), can also be labeled as confounding variables. Indeed, when they are controlled, the effects of contingent pay on well-being outcomes are reduced. That is precisely the major limitation of nonexperimental studies: performance-contingent pay plans, especially piece rate, tend to be used more on jobs that are repetitive and potentially monotonous, and such jobs also tend to be the most stressful (Caplan, Cobb, French, Harrison, & Pinneau, 1975).

Research on performance-contingent pay and stress has focused mostly on blue-collar, industrial jobs. In contrast, occupations that often employ performance-based pay plans are increasingly white collar, and even professional. Researchers should begin to concentrate on a wider range of occupations. Many types of sales positions, for example, use performance-based pay, yet they do not appear in the stress literature. Recent calls to hold professionals such as teachers (e.g., see Springer et al., 2010) and health care workers (e.g., see Rosenthal & Dudley, 2007) more accountable by making their pay contingent on performance suggest other interesting contexts for studying the stress effects of performance-based pay.

Understanding the causal mechanisms underlying the effects of performance-based pay requires much closer attention to the mediating and moderating variables involved in this relationship. For example, the impact of one's pay plan is likely mediated by the cognitive appraisals of the worker, and this evokes several questions for future research. How do such performance-based plans, or what aspects of such plans, evoke appraisals of threat? Are any stress effects of such pay plans caused by a lowering of control beliefs, income uncertainty, or disrupted social factors triggered by such plans in the workplace? None of these hypothesized factors have been systematically studied. Given the highly salient impacts of reward systems in organizational settings, they provide a rich opportunity to better understand the factors that have a significant impact on worker stress and well-being.

REFERENCES

Brief, A. P., & Atieh, J. M. (1987). Studying job stress: Are we making mountains out of molehills? *Journal of Occupational Behaviour, 8,* 115–126.

Brisson, C., Vinet, A., Vézina, M., & Gingras, S. (1989). Effect of duration of employment in piecework on severe disability among female garment workers. *Scandinavian Journal of Work Environmental Health, 15,* 329–334.

Caplan, R. D., Cobb, S., French, J. R. P., Jr., Harrison, R. V., & Pinneau, S. R. (1975). *Job demands and worker health* (U. S. Department of Health, Education, and Welfare, Publication No. 75-160). Washington, DC: National Institute for Occupational Safety and Health.

Deci, E. L. (1975). *Intrinsic motivation.* New York, NY: Plenum.

Deci, E. L., & Ryan, R. M. (1987). The support of autonomy and the control of behavior. *Journal of Personality and Social Psychology, 53,* 1024–1037.

Duncan, P. K, & Smoot, D. T. (2001). Pay for performance. In C. M. Johnson, W. K. Redmon, & T. C. Mawhinney (Eds.), *Handbook of organizational performance: Behavior analysis and management* (pp. 255–276). New York, NY: Haworth.

Eisenberger, R., Rhoades, L., & Cameron, J. (1999). Does pay for performance increase or decrease perceived self-determination and intrinsic motivation? *Journal of Personality and Social Psychology, 77,* 1026–1040.

Folkman, S., & Lazarus, R. S. (1990). Coping and emotion. In N. L. Stein, B. Leventhal, & T. Trabasso (Eds.), *Psychological and biological approaches to emotion* (pp. 313–332). Hillsdale, NJ: Erlbaum.

Friedman, M. D., Rosenman, R. D., & Carroll, V. (1958). Changes in serum cholesterol and blood clotting time in men subjected to cyclic variation of occupational stress. *Circulation, 17,* 852–861.

Frisch, C. J., & Dickinson, A. M. (1990). Work productivity as a function of the percentage of monetary incentives to base pay. *Journal of Organizational Behavior Management, 11*(1), 13–33.

Ganster, D. C., & Fusilier, M. R. (1989). Control in the work place. In C. L. Cooper & I. T. Robinson (Eds.), *International review of Industrial and Organizational Psychology* (pp. 235–280). New York, NY: Wiley.

Hewitt and Associates. (2004, June 9). Many companies fail to achieve success with pay-for-performance programs. *News & Information.*

Houlfort, N., Koestner, R., Joussemet, M., Nantel-Viver, A., & Lekes, N. (2002). The impact of performance-contingent rewards on perceived autonomy and competence. *Motivation and Emotion, 26,* 279–295.

Howard, L. W., & Dougherty, T. W. (2004). Alternative reward strategies and employee reactions. *Compensation & Benefits Review, 36*, 41–51.

Jenkins, G. D, Jr., Mitra, A., Gupta, N., & Shaw, J. D. (1998). Are financial incentives related to performance? *A meta-analytic review of empirical research. Journal of Applied Psychology, 83*, 777–787.

Kahn, R. L. (1981). *Work and health.* New York, NY: Wiley.

Kain, J., & Jex, S. (2010). Karasek's (1979) job demands-control model: A summary of current issues and recommendations for future research. In P. Perrewé & D. C. Ganster (Eds.), *Research in occupational stress and well being, Volume 8: New developments in theoretical and conceptual approaches to job stress* (pp. 237–268). Bingley, England: Emerald.

Karasek, R. (1979). Job demands, job decision latitude, and mental strain: Implications for job redesign. *Administrative Science Quarterly, 24*, 285–307.

Karasek R., & Theorell, T. (1990). *Healthy work.* New York, NY: Basic Books.

Kurdelbusch, A. (2002). Multinationals and the rise of variable pay in Germany. *European Journal of Industrial Relations, 8*, 325–349.

Lawler, E. E. (1990). *Strategic pay.* San Francisco, CA: Jossey-Bass.

Levi, L. (1972). Conditions of work and sympathoadrenomedullary activity: Experimental manipulations in a real life setting. *Acta Medica Scandinavia, 191*, 106–118.

Muraven, M., Rosman, H., & Gagné, M. (2007). Lack of autonomy and self-control: Performance contingent rewards lead to greater depletion. *Motivation and Emotion, 31*, 322–330.

NIOSH (1999). *Stress at work* (U.S. National Institute for Occupational Safety and Health, DHHS [NIOSH] Publication No. 99-101). Washington, DC: Author. Retrieved from http://www.cdc.gov/niosh/docs/99-101/

Perrewé, P. L., & Ganster, D. C. (Eds.) (2010). *Research in occupational stress and well being. Volume 8: New developments in theoretical, conceptual, and methodological approaches to job stress.* Bingley, England: Emerald.

Pfeffer, J. (2007). Human resources from an organizational behavior perspective: Some paradoxes explained. *Journal of Economic Perspectives, 21*, 115–134.

Pfeffer, J., & Langton, N. (1993). The effect of wage dispersion on satisfaction, productivity, and working collaboratively: Evidence from college and university faculty. *Administrative Science Quarterly, 38*, 382–407.

Quick, J. C., & Tetrick, L. E. (2011). *Handbook of occupational health psychology* (2nd ed.). Washington, DC: American Psychological Association.

Rosenthal, M. B., & Dudley, R. A. (2007). Pay-for-performance: Will the latest trend improve care? *Journal of the American Medical Association, 297*, 740–744.

Ryan, R. M., & Deci, E. L. (2000). Self-determination theory and the facilitation of intrinsic motivation, social development, and well-being. *American Psychologist, 55*, 68–78.

Shirom, A., Westman, M., & Melamed, S. (1999). The effects of pay systems on blue-collar employees' emotional distress: The mediating effects of objective and subjective work monotony. *Human Relations, 52*, 1077–1097.

Smith, M. J., Carayon, P., Sanders, K. J., Lim, S.-Y., & LeGrande, D. (1992). Employee stress and health complaints in jobs with and without electronic performance monitoring. *Applied Ergonomics, 23*, 17–27.

Springer, M. G., Ballou, D., Hamilton, L., Le, V., Lockwood, J. R., McCaffrey, D., . . . Stecher, B. (2010). *Teacher pay for performance: Experimental evidence from the Project on Incentives in Teaching*. Nashville, TN: National Center on Performance Incentives at Vanderbilt University.

Stordeur, S., D'Hoore, W., & Vandenberghe, C. (2001). Leadership, organizational stress, and emotional exhaustion among hospital nursing staff. *Journal of Advanced Nursing, 35*, 533–542.

Timio, M., and Gentili, S. (1976). Adrenosympathetic overactivity under conditions of work stress. *British Journal of Preventive and Social Medicine, 30*, 262–265.

Timio, M., Gentili, S., & Pede, S. (1979). Free adrenaline and noradrenaline excretion related to occupational stress. *British Heart Journal, 42*, 471–474.

Williams, C. R., & Livingstone, L. P. (1994). Another look at the relationship between performance and voluntary turnover. *Academy of Management Journal, 37*, 269–298.

Yeh, W., Cheng, Y., & Chen, C. (2009). Social patterns of pay systems and their associations with psychosocial job characteristics and burnout among paid employees in Taiwan. *Social Science & Medicine, 68*, 1407–1415.

Yoder, D. (1947). *Personnel management and industrial relations*. New York, NY: Prentice-Hall.

Promoting Critical Operant-Based Leadership While Decreasing Ubiquitous Directives and Exhortations

JUDITH L. KOMAKI, MICHELLE L. R. MINNICH, ANGELA R. GROTTO, BRET WEINSHANK, and MICHAEL J. KERN
Baruch College, CUNY, New York, New York, USA

Equipping leaders to successfully motivate their teams is daunting, especially when the prevailing management practice is to simply tell people what to do. Training based on the theoretically and empirically based Operant Model of Effective Supervision was provided to seasoned managers in the private and public sectors. A randomized posttest-only design was used. Trainees responded in their own words to diverse true-to-life scenarios in an in-basket assessment. In both settings, training not only increased the newly learned skills of monitoring and providing positive/neutral consequences, but it also reduced lackluster antecedent-only strategies.

[Supplementary materials are available for this article. Go to the publisher's online edition of *Journal of Organizational Behavior Management* for the following free supplemental resource: Table: Additional Managerial Training Experiments in the I/O Literature.]

Effectively motivating employees remains a challenge (Steers & Porter, 1990). But just as daunting is equipping leaders to successfully lead their teams in a productive and harmonious fashion (Campbell, Dunnette, Lawler, & Weick, 1970). Assuming that leaders are largely responsible for creating the motivational atmospheres within their units, how do we best ensure that they do what they need to do? Perhaps just as essential, how do we help managers avoid lackluster practices?

As behavior analysts, we know that simply telling people what to do is not the best way to motivate people. Yet, when confronted with problems involving the work force, giving directives and exhortations are common management practices. Often managers "inform or exhort, or both" (Mager & Pipe, 1984, p. 1). Daniels (2000) captures the dilemma well: "We send memos, have meetings, write policies, hold classes, and make informational and inspirational speeches." Unfortunately, when the directives and exhortations do not have the effect we want, we often tell the same folks all over again in much the same way, "only this time we tell them a little louder, or a little longer, or perhaps a little meaner" (p. 17).

Unique in the social sciences, operant conditioning identifies two major concepts depending on the time at which they occur: (a) antecedents such as directives, exhortations, and goals that typically precede the targeted behavior; and (b) consequences such as feedback that takes place after performance. Consequences are the major motivational force. Antecedents fulfill valuable educational and cuing functions, but not a primary motivational one. Daniels (2000) puts it succinctly: "Antecedents get us going: consequences keep us going" (p. 22). A laboratory simulation of a work setting showed that antecedents such as persuasive influence or announcements alone were insufficient to increase and sustain performance. Instead, performance improved only when a pay contingency was put into place (Johnson, 1975). Furthermore, time-series designs conducted in multiple work settings showed that antecedents alone do not result in substantial improvements and that only when consequences accompany antecedents do dramatic changes occur. Komaki, Heinzmann, and Lawson (1980), for example, found that employees receiving antecedents in the form of a slide presentation, verbal explanations, and written rules only slightly increased their performance. Not until feedback was provided did performance substantially improve.

Yet, antecedent strategies are prevalent throughout the I/O leadership literature. Initiating the structure of the task is one of two major dimensions in the classic Ohio State Studies (Fleishman, 1973). Antecedents such as the inspirational speeches and confidently-worded expectations of performance are integral to transformational leadership theory (Bass, 1985; House, 1977). Probably the most highly regarded work motivation theory emphasizes the antecedent, goal-setting (Locke & Latham, 1990). Given the highlighting and prevalence of antecedents, a pressing question remains: how do we help leaders to go beyond telling people what to do and why to do it?

OPERANT MODEL OF EFFECTIVE SUPERVISION EMPHASIZES PERFORMANCE MONITORS AND CONSEQUENCES, BUT DOWNPLAYS RELYING ON ANTECEDENTS

The Operant Model of Effective Supervision (Komaki, 1998) seeks to identify what effective leaders really need to do to motivate others every day, every season. Inspired by the theory of operant conditioning, the Model focuses on what occurs *after* the performance of the worker. Hence, Komaki (1998) highlights the providing of performance *consequences*. Effective managers have been seen to provide positive ("Thanks for the feedback. . . . Your program is important to the company and we need to figure out how to facilitate it."), neutral ("I'll talk to Carl and get back to you."), and negative ("Sorry to hear about the mix-up, but [something doesn't] match.") consequences.

Because consequences need to be related to performance, Komaki (1998) conjectured that effective managers would frequently *monitor* or inquire about performance. The original rationale was logical—managers who monitor are more likely to have dependable and up-to-date information with which to provide contingent consequences. One can gather information via self-report ("Have you discussed the form with Terry?") or, even better as exemplary managers have done, by directly sampling the work ("I'd like to see those forms so I can make an informed decision.").

EVIDENCE EXISTS IN THE MODEL FOR MONITORING AND PROVIDING CONSEQUENCES

In eight field studies done in connection with the Model, effective managers monitored, provided consequences, or did both (Komaki, 1998[1]). Exemplary police sergeants went beyond telling officers what to do and instead spent more time monitoring verbal reports on patrol activities and providing consequences considered neutral. Monitoring was done by highly rated insurance managers more often than their lackluster counterparts. These exemplary managers checked on quality by work sampling, watching workers at their computers, or picking up and examining claim forms. Construction supervisors, rated highly by their own work crews, gave consequences that were positive, neutral, and negative. Consequences sometimes were as brief as a simple "thanks" or even an "okay" said while sampling the work. Winning sailboat skippers used a particular sequence during races, with monitors routinely preceding consequences in what is referred to as an AMC sequence, where "A" stands for Antecedent, "M" for Monitor, and "C" for Consequence,

---

[1] Please refer to Komaki (1998) for detailed discussions of seven of the eight field studies conducted by Komaki et al., Brewer et al., and Niehoff and Moorman. Due to space limitations, they are not referenced. The eighth study by Reynard Minnich, Komaki, and Donovan (2004) is referenced.

with exemplary leaders doing these AMC sequences quickly. A particular type of positive consequence, thanking the bearer of bad news in which employees were acknowledged for bringing thorny issues to their managers' attention, was done more often by well-rated investment bankers (Reynard Minnich, Komaki, & Donovan, 2004). These eight studies conducted by research teams in Australia, Finland, and the U.S. include criteria of leader effectiveness ranging from ratings by superiors and subordinates to outcome measures such as win-loss records.

ANTECEDENTS PLAY A SECONDARY ROLE IN THE MODEL

Since the Model's inception, antecedents have been relegated to a secondary role. Effective managers were not expected to stop at setting goals or expectations. In order to sustain performance, they were predicted to go beyond antecedents to monitor and provide consequences.

Tests of the Model confirmed their secondary role. Neither the quantity nor quality of antecedents was predictive of exemplary leaders (Komaki, 1998). Seven of eight tests found antecedents did not distinguish between effective and lackluster managers.[2] One study, done in a daily newspaper operation, found antecedents were a suppressor; that is, effective managers were able to raise the level of consequences without necessarily increasing the level of antecedents. Even when antecedents were divided by subcategories (e.g., specificity, delivery), no relationships were found with effectiveness.

OPPORTUNITIES AROSE TO TRAIN SEASONED LEADERS IN PRIVATE AND PUBLIC SECTORS

Managers in two settings, a merchandising company and the Emergency Medical Service (EMS) of a city fire department, were recruited and trained. With EMS managers, the concern was that people and procedures need to be in place when emergencies arise. Getting personnel to go out on calls is not a problem; in fact, on September 11, 2001, a rash of Fire Department of New York (FDNY) and other emergency personnel who were off duty voluntarily showed up to aid victims. The difficulty lies in motivating personnel to properly complete everyday routines in preparation for emergencies: maintaining the defibrillator battery charger and putting batteries back in the charger so that when paramedics need it to "jump start" the heart of a patient, it is ready. "Getting ready" is what military personnel in peacetime

---

[2] The only study in which antecedents were related to effectiveness, $r = -.40, p < .05$, was conducted in a three-member team that had not previously worked together, with one of the members a neophyte. Because of the inexperience of one of the members and the lack of seasoning of the team, it was not unexpected that effective leaders would spend more time than usual telling people what to do.

spend "100% of their time" doing (Salas, Milham, & Bowers, 2003, p. 14). Similarly, in the private sector, these routine but vital tasks, which leadership specialist Sayles (1979) refers to as "housekeeping," are tough for leaders to successfully sustain. Hence, we were delighted to train seasoned managers in both the private and the public sectors.

EVALUATING EFFECTIVENESS OF TRAINING USING AN IN-BASKET ASSESSMENT

As much as $125.9 billion is estimated to have been spent on employee learning and development in the U. S. alone (Patel, 2010). Unfortunately, training is seldom evaluated. Reviewers of the training literature bemoan the scarcity and quality of the evaluations. Wexley (1984) noted how he intended to have a section on management development, but finally eliminated it because "so little research has been conducted on this topic" (p. 521). In 2001, Salas and Canon-Bowers were still calling for "more documentation" (p. 473). More recently, Salas (2010), after reviewing 1,502 studies from 1980–2006 military training programs on teams, concluded that although there have been short-term gains in effective interpersonal relations, it has had little effect on performance outcomes.

Not surprisingly, an extensive search of the literature yielded only seven published experiments aimed at improving employee productivity and/or leaders' supervisory skills (Table 1).[3] Training ranged from general management principles to specific leadership theories (e.g., transformational), with one on the Model (Methot, Williams, Cummings, & Bradshaw, 1996).

Methods for assessing leaders' supervisory skills include questionnaires, vignettes, simulations, observations, and in-basket assessments. The methods differ in terms of the quality of the stimuli presented to the trainee—from "canned" issues to surrogate/live interactions—as well as the nature of their response—from multiple choice formats to demonstrating via their own actions and words in situ (Table 2).

The most prevalent method, the *questionnaire*, suffers from problems with both stimuli and response. Trainees are typically presented with generic problem statements (e.g., handling a complaining employee). Responses are limited, e.g., reporting the frequency or the extent to which they have performed—from "never, not a lot" to "always, to a very great extent."

With *vignettes*, the scenarios presented are relatively plentiful (e.g., from 8 to 22), but they often pose "canned," easily digestible and apparent issues

---

[3] Go to the publisher's online edition of *Journal of Organizational Behavior Management* for a supplemental table—Additional Managerial Training Experiments in the I/O Literature—that includes descriptions of 26 experiments evaluating training aimed at improving employees' attitudes (e.g., self-efficacy), managers' performance appraisal skills, as well as aspects ranging from employee assistance programs to union-management relations. The extended table can also be found on the OBM Network website and newsletter.

INTEGRATING OBM WITH I/O PSYCHOLOGY

(e.g., someone who insists that orders be carried out within a specified time limit but fails to check if employee is meeting the deadlines). Responses range from writing down what they would do to choosing among possible responses in a multiple-choice format. Hence, problems exist with the stimuli and in some cases, the responses.

TABLE 1 Experiments Evaluating Managerial Training Aimed at Improving Employee Productivity and/or Managers' Supervisory Skills

Exp.	Sample Description	N	Training Content	Criteria
1	Bank branch managers	20	Implementing transformational leadership theory concepts	Questionnaires measuring subordinate perceptions of managers' transformational leadership and subordinate organizational commitment, branch-level personal loan and credit card sales
2	Squad leaders	54	Transformational leadership (motivation, morality, and empowerment)	Follower development: self-actualization techniques, internalization of organizational moral values, collectivistic orientation, active engagement, and self-efficacy; follower performance: objective tests of technical or physical skills
3	Form-processing employees of public organization	106	LMX and job design	Satisfaction and productivity before-and-after gains
4	Managers of large municipal government	33	Improvement of managers' interactions with their natural work groups	Systematic Multiple Level Observation of Groups Leadership Values Instrument to measure group and individual effectiveness
5	First-line supervisors and managers in consumer product manufacturing plant	38	Four active listening skills to equip supervisors for facilitative role in team environment (act like a listener, establish and maintain rapport, ask open-ended questions, and check for understanding)	Immediate knowledge, knowledge retention, pre- and postbehavior/skill demonstration with a videotaped role-play, pre- and postlistening practices questionnaire, transfer of training, and feedback/interviews

(Continued)

TABLE 1 (Continued)

Exp.	Sample Description	N	Training Content	Criteria
6	Managers, supervisors, direct care staff, and clients of employment training center and residential facility	28	Model of effective supervision (e.g., behavioral components of feedback meetings, objective monitoring of staff performance)	Interactions of managers and supervisors with clients about target behaviors
7	Managers from several units/ departments in insurance company	14	Planning, problem solving, motivating direct reports, communication, leadership, delegation, performance appraisals, and administrative procedures	Trainees' opinions about job-relatedness and effectiveness of training, skill acquisition self-report questionnaire, employees' observation of management-trained behaviors, work unit performance pre- and posttraining

Note. References: Exp. 1, Barling, Weber, and Kelloway (1996); Exp. 2, Dvir, Eden, Avolio, and Shamir (2002); Exp. 3, Graen, Novak, and Sommerkamp (1982); Exp. 4, Lawrence and Wiswell (1993); Exp. 5, May and Kahnweiler (2000); Exp. 6, Methot, Williams, Cummings, and Bradshaw (1996); Exp. 7, Paquet, Kasl, Weinstein, and Waite (1987).

TABLE 2 Format of Dependent Variables Assessing Motivational Skills of Trainees: Questionnaires, Vignettes, and Simulations[1]

	Format of dependent variables[2]	
	Stimulus	Response
	Questionnaire[3]	
Exp.	Trainees filled out generic questionnaire:	Trainees responded:
1	E.g., emphasizing improvement and discussing advancement[4] 12 behaviors	By noting the extent to which they displayed the behaviors, ranging from 1 (*highly agree*) to 9 (*highly disagree*).[5] To researcher
2	E.g., planning, problem solving, motivating direct reports, communication, leadership, and delegation 6 behaviors	By indicating the extent to which they acquired a skill, ranging from 1 (most positive) to 5 (most negative) To researcher
3	E.g., motivating a person to problem solve, handling a complaining employee 4 learning points	By indicating the frequency of a behavior on the job for the past four months, ranging from 1 (*almost always*) to 5 (*almost never*). To researcher
4	E.g., ". . .meets regularly with other associates to discuss problem and identify ways to solve them." 18 behaviors	By identifying the extent to which they performed a behavior on the job, ranging from 1 (*never, not at all*) to 5 (*always, to a very great*). To researcher

(Continued)

TABLE 2 (Continued)

	Vignette	
Exp.	Trainees responded to vignettes:	Trainees responded:
5	Composed of typical problems with subordinates (e.g., "Insists that orders be carried out within a specified time limit & check to be sure he is meeting those deadlines.") 8 vignettes	By rating four possible responses on how characteristic each is of what they would do and prescribing a solution To researcher
6	Based on actual incidents of problems, (e.g., "One of your employees has recently been using too many tool bits... He has three years seniority... and has been a satisfactory performer.") 22 vignettes	By acting as foreman and writing about what they would do To researcher

	Simulation	
Exp.	Trainees participated in simulations:	Trainees responded:
7	Based on situations deemed relevant and realistic by senior management (e.g., requiring them to take on a facilitative role in a team environment) 2 simulations, 8 minutes each	By role-playing With a surrogate
8	Based on three common scenarios: 1) parent-initiated teacher conference, 2) principal-initiated teacher conference, and 3) principal-initiated group discussion with four faculty members[6] 3 simulations	By role-playing With a surrogate

Note. References: Exp. 1, Dorfman, Stephan, and Loveland (1986); Exp. 2, Paquet et al. (1987); Exp. 3, Russell et al. (1984); Exp. 4, Tracey, Tannenbaum, and Kavanagh (1995); Exp. 5, Deci, Connell, and Ryan (1989); Exp. 6, Russell, Wexley, and Hunter (1984); Exp. 7, May and Kahnweiler (2000); Exp. 8, Smith, White, and Montello (1992).
[1]Studies from Dvir et al. (2002); Graen et al. (1982); Scandura and Graen (1984) were not included because no assessment was made of trainees' skills.
[2]Observations were used for the dependent variable in Methot et al. (1996). Trainees were observed for two 20-minute periods per week for up to 34 weeks on monitors and related contingent consequences.
[3]A questionnaire was used in another study (Lawrence & Wiswell, 1993), but full information was unavailable.
[4]Trainees also filled out satisfaction and motivation questionnaires.
[5]Trainees responded by indicating their degree of satisfaction and motivation on a 5-point scale.
[6]One group of trainees participated in these three simulations and a different group participated in one simulated feedback interview with a teacher.

In a *simulation*, trainees take on a role, interact with a surrogate and demonstrate how they would respond, e.g., in a simulated parent-teacher conference. The quality of the response is good. The problem is that trainees engage in only two or three simulations, calling into question the breadth of the situations in which they can apply what they have learned.

Observations have similar pros and cons as simulations. In one of the few supervisory training evaluations using observations, Methot et al. (1996) actually observed manager-to-supervisor, supervisor-to-staff, and staff-to-client interactions. Though the observations were extensive with five observers each coding two 20-minute periods a week for up to 34 weeks, they were limited by necessity to prescribed interactions. Hence, it was not clear how broadly trainees could exhibit the skills (e.g., in less formal situations with peers). Furthermore, questions arose about the feasibility of evaluating training using such a labor-intensive method.

Another promising alternative, rarely if ever used, is the *in-basket assessment* (Schippman, Prien, & Katz, 1990). Trainees are confronted with scenarios covering myriad topics, power positions, and personalities, and they respond in whatever way they choose. To gather information on the Model's behaviors, Komaki (1998) created an in-basket, called the Motivational Effectiveness Exercise (MEE). It includes 21 scenarios, ranging from routine reports to impassioned pleas about flagrant problems. Respondents take approximately an hour to complete the MEE, choosing whom they wish to respond to and replying in their own words.

Given the MEE, it was possible to test the hypothesis that managers trained to monitor and provide positive/neutral consequences will increase these behaviors. As an exploratory probe, we could also assess whether they decreased antecedents used to promote motivation. Our interest was in whether trained managers would be more or less likely when faced with a problem to rely on directives or exhortations alone for motivation.

METHOD

Subjects and Settings

Experiment 1 was conducted in a family-owned merchandising agency. With over 150 employees, the company manufactures retail displays and fixtures. Both the president and the general manager, contacted by Bret Weinshank, thought the training might be helpful and well-received. The trainees consisted of 12 lower- to upper-level managers who ranged from assistant to vice president and were concerned with development, design, creative, engineering, production, accounting, and sales.

The EMS Operations unit of a major metropolitan fire department was the site of Experiment 2. Covering over 300 square miles, the unit dispatches its personnel each year to over 1 million assignments and provides services ranging from basic and advanced life support to hazardous materials operations. The Chief of EMS was interested in how managers could best manage employees to respond quickly to ambulance calls and provide quality care. Trainees consisted of 63 managers, including lieutenants (40), captains (17), and deputy chiefs and a division commander (6).

Participants signed a consent form permitting the use of their data for research purposes.

Design and Procedures

A posttest-only control group design with stratified random sampling was used. Taking into consideration the rank of the individuals, participants were randomly assigned to treatment or control groups—in Exp. 1, 7 and 5 persons, and in Exp. 2, 32 and 31 persons, respectively.[4]

Training was given to the treatment groups by the first author. It took place in Exp. 1 over 8 hours, broken down into 2-hour sessions held weekly over 4 weeks. For Exp. 2, it was by necessity given in five hours during a single day.

The Motivational Effectiveness Exercise (MEE) was taken by all. In Exp. 1, both groups took the MEE a week after the treatment group completed training. In Exp. 2, the control group took the MEE before training (on the Model by the second author) and the treatment group after training.

Dependent Variable: Motivational Effectiveness Exercise

An in-basket exercise, the MEE, was used to measure supervisory behaviors in simulated settings. Respondents took on the role of a food magazine publisher and responded to memos found in their "in-basket" from employees and department directors. Memos varied by topic, personality of sender, and urgency of message. Respondents were encouraged to address each memo, to reply to whomever they wished in whatever way they saw fit and, rather than setting up a meeting, to indicate what they would actually say to the person during the meeting. They were given 60 minutes to finish.

Evidence exists for the convergent and divergent validity of the MEE (Komaki et al., 1990). Behaviors of computer managers measured via simulation were correlated with the same behaviors assessed via observation on the job (monitors, $r = .57$; consequences, $r = .60$); monitors were not related to consequences, even when the same method was used.

CATEGORIES AND SUBCATEGORIES

Three categories of behavior were scored, monitoring, providing consequences, and antecedents (Table 3). Monitoring was divided by method (via *work sampling* and *self-report*); antecedents by type (*relying on for motivation* and *tacking-on traditional antecedents*); and consequences by

---

[4] Control and treatment groups in both samples did not differ significantly in demographic characteristics such as age, years of education, and supervisory experience. The only significant difference was in EMS participants' self-rated motivational skills, with the treatment group rating themselves higher than the control group.

sign (*negative* and *positive/neutral*). Positive consequences were further broken into (a) providing *simple*, short acknowledgements for standard reports ("Thanks for the info."); (b) giving *traditional* positives for effort or accomplishments ("I appreciate the efforts you made in providing . . . trainees with [attachment]."); (c) *thanking the bearer of bad news* ("Thanks for going the extra mile to [resolve the situation]."); (d) *acknowledging someone out of the contact loop* (to an outside contractor, "I understand there was a problem in filling out the . . . form. Is there anything you might think needs to be changed? Your input is very valuable to me."); and (e) *broadcasting* congratulations *to multiple parties* ("Well done!!! Let me congratulate you on an outstanding year. Keep up the great work."). Two neutral consequences considered neither positive nor negative[5] were included: (a) *letting the sender/other(s) know of action taken* ("I've addressed your concerns with [Dept. C] and will do my best to correct the problem."); and (b) *relaying* a *problem nonjudgmentally* ("I heard there was a problem. . . . Please let me know if I can help to solve this problem. I asked Tim to [provide additional assistance].").

Giving antecedents, defined as conveying expectations of performance, were broken into two types: giving *tacked-on traditional antecedents* and *using antecedents for motivation*. The latter were delivered in the absence of monitors or consequences as exhortations or persuasions in an attempt to try and motivate persons. When notified of a customer criticism, for example, a respondent did not try to verify if the criticism was accurate or get more information on the situation, but merely sent the following message: "I know you have a difficult job, but we simply cannot afford to lose one of our largest accounts. Kindly instruct your employees to [perform as instructed] promptly and courteously at all times!".

SCORING

The five authors did the scoring. All were kept blind to the identity of respondents and group to which they were assigned. Responses to each item were scored category by category and subcategory by subcategory. As many as six points could be given per item for a consequence, and as many as six for a monitor. More points were awarded for higher quality responses, e.g., the subcategory of monitoring via work sampling counted for more than self-report. A response to an item could contain multiple categories. When a manager provided a positive/neutral consequence and a monitor, points were given for both categories. Hence, a response could be awarded 12 points, 6 for the highest quality monitor and 6 for the highest quality positive/neutral consequence.

---

[5] These neutral consequences fit the definition of a consequence because they showed knowledge of the message received or the target's performance.

TABLE 3 Categories and Subcategories of Behavior in the Motivational Effectiveness Exercise (MEE): Definitions and Examples

CATEGORY/ Subcategory	Definition	Examples		
		MEE item 1[a] Complaint from employee in Dept. A about difficulty with a new form devised by Dept. B	MEE item 2 Relay of client criticism about service in Dept. C	MEE item 3 Concern expressed by employee of Dept. D about the shoddy work of Dept. E
MONITORING	Gathering information about performance			
Work sample	Indicating interest in observing workers in action and/or examining work products	*Please forward a copy of both the old and new forms to me, I will review.*	*I would like you to personally visit the department . . . [and] to call . . . . . See how you are treated and then report back to me and we will discuss it further.*	*I will be meeting with [Dept. E Mgr.] . . . Send me the sample of [work] in question.*
Self-report	Asking person for more information about performance	*Please let me know about what changes have been made in the new . . . forms—were the changes necessary and were instructions sent out with the new forms?*	*[To Dept. C Dir.] [A client] is very angry. . . . Note: While I am aware of the complaint, is there any reason to believe it is true? Who is handling their account?*	*[To Dept. E Dir.] Is there a problem with [work in] your department? Please confer with [Dept. E Mgr.] [about it].*

(*Continued*)

TABLE 3 (Continued)

		MEE item 2 Relay of client criticism about service in Dept. C	MEE item 4 Material sent with mistake	MEE item 5 Discussion by Dept. F's Dir. about Dept. G's lack of follow through, including misleading attachment
PROVIDING CONSEQUENCES		Communicating knowledge of performance		
Positive	Recognizing accomplishment or effort	*Thanks for bringing me up to speed on this. I will call [client] myself to assure them that their concerns are important to us....*	*The [material] look[s] good. The [error] I'm not so sure. Stop the presses!*	*I appreciate the efforts you made in providing ... trainees with [attachment]. However there is a bit of confusion when reviewing [it].*
Neutral	Expressing neither approval nor disapproval of performance	*...I've addressed your concerns with [Dept. C] and will do my best to correct the problem...*	—	*[To Dept. G Dir.] I heard there was a problem.... Please let me know if I can help to solve this problem. I asked [Dept. F Dir.] to [provide additional assistance].*
Negative	Pointing out error seen first-hand, but in a way that is not sarcastic, abrupt, or demeaning	—	*Hold up! You have a [mistake]. [described] Please ...review.... These can be costly mistakes and I am sure you can see, unprofessional.*	*Pardon me if I point out to you the [error in your attachment]. I can see where [Dept. G] could have had a problem.*

	MEE item 2 Relay of client criticism about service in Dept. C	MEE item 4 Material sent with mistake	MEE item 6 Employee provides status report on preparations
PROVIDING ANTECEDENTS	Conveying expectations of performance via directives, instructions, reminders, exhortations, or persuasions		
Tacking on traditional antecedents	[Dept. C Dir.] will need to handle him directly. [She] should call immediately and give them her pager and cell numbers.	As a suggestion, how about adding color and something to call attention to [it]?	OK [sender], let's keep it up, like you said, "Two short months away!" [To sender's Dept. Dir.] [memo sender] updated me on the [project]. Time is running short, maybe you need to get [employee name] and [employee name 2] some help. We need these tasks finalized by the end of this week please. Update me Friday morning.
Using antecedents for motivation	[To Dept. C Dir.] We have received a complaint. . . . The client claims [problems with] the service. Plz review the company policies with your employees if they need more training. . . . Plz contact [HR] to set up training times. We need to keep this client happy. Thanks!!!	[To sender's Dept. Dir.] [memo sender] is sending her [material] along. Please have your staff make sure everything is spelled correctly before we print. Check twice, print once makes it a better job.	—

Note. [a]Each MEE item is paraphrased so as to avoid items being immediately recognized, and worthy answers quoted verbatim, hence compromising the integrity of future results.

Overall category scores were calculated by summing subcategory scores across items (e.g., monitoring overall consisted of the sum of work sample and self-report) for each participant, and then dividing by the total number of points possible for the category and multiplying by 100, to yield a percentage score. For example, if a respondent received 17 points for monitoring via work sampling and 11 points for self-report, the overall raw monitoring score would be 28 points. Monitoring was possible on 12 items in the MEE, for a total of 66 points possible, so the respondent's monitoring score would be calculated as 28 divided by 66 and multiplied by 100, for a score of 42%.

INTERRATER AGREEMENT

Scoring was done independently. Every response was scored by two people, enabling interrater agreement scores to be calculated not on a sample, but on all responses. Any disagreements were discussed and reconciled by consensus agreement.

Interrater agreement, calculated as (# of agreements / # of total × 100), was a percentage score. An agreement was counted when both scorers coded the same category or subcategory. For categories, the denominator of the formula, or total, was the number of categories coded by the primary scorer (PS).[6] Hence, when scorers agreed on 9 monitors out of a total of 10 identified by the PS, the agreement score for monitoring would be 90%. For subcategories, the total was the number of categories agreed to by both scorers. When there were 8 agreements for method of monitoring out of a total of 9, the agreement score would be 8 out of 9, or 88.9%.

In Exp. 1, the overall percentage agreement score was 84.6%. Scores for monitoring, providing positive/neutral consequences, and providing antecedents ranged from 82% to 92%, within the limits of acceptability (80%) for a new measure (Miller, 1997). Agreement for negative consequences (75%) was slightly below the acceptable limit. In Exp. 2, the overall percentage agreement score was 77.2%. Agreement for positive/neutral consequences was 83%. Scores for antecedents, monitoring, and negative consequences ranged from 71% to 77%.

Independent Variable: Training Based on Operant Model of Effective Supervision

Training covered the Model's behaviors of monitors and consequences. After soliciting trainee's ideas for optimal leader behaviors and then describing

---

[6] For Exp. 1, the first and second authors were PS, and the third and fifth authors were the other scorers. For Exp. 2, the second author was the PS and the fourth author the other scorer.

the rationale and evidence for the Model, the topic of monitoring was introduced: its definition, the conditions under which it is best to monitor, the different methods, and examples. Consequences followed: its definition, the different types of positive and neutral consequences, and examples. Examples were drawn from a variety of settings; in Exp. 2, for instance, job-specific examples were gleaned from interviews with EMS supervisors identified as exemplary.[7] In Exp. 1, negative consequences were presented as well with emphasis on paying attention to detail and being diplomatic in delivery.

Active participation was encouraged throughout with ensuing lively discussions. Trainees were asked to recognize examples ("Is this manager providing a [neutral] consequence?"), distinguish between different types of behaviors ("Is this a work sample or self-report?"), discuss where they may have already used the skills on the job ("Anyone ever thank the bearer of bad news?"), and identify where the skills could be fruitfully applied ("Any other report you could use to monitor performance?").

Ample practice and feedback were built into the training. Because training took place over four weeks in Exp. 1, homework was assigned. Trainees went back to their jobs and applied the principles; they monitored performance in week 1, and in week 2 they provided positive/neutral consequences. The following week, each trainee discussed his or her experiences, both good and bad, with a rapt, sometimes cheering audience of their peers. Furthermore, practice was provided in both Exp. 1 and 2 with true-to-life scenarios. Trainees filled out in-basket items, similar to those in the MEE, in which they were the principal of a high school. They then saw how others had responded to the same in-basket item. To help them see how they already were using the Model's behaviors, the instructor asked, "Any one monitor work sample here? A show of hands? Willing to read your response? What did you think of that one? Anyone else work sample?" In addition, in Exp. 2, the EMS managers analyzed cases of actual managers grappling with problems in a school, a newspaper office, and an Iraqi prison camp ("What's the principal doing right according to the Model? How is the publisher monitoring the accuracy of the reporting?"). Based on their analyses, trainees were asked to build on what was being done well and offer suggestions based on the Model ("How would you point out to the officer in charge what she was doing right? How would you make suggestions to the officer to ensure prisoners were treated humanely?").

---

[7] One fairly elaborate but subtle example took place after a difficult call in which a new medication had been used. The paramedic unit came back to discuss the call with a well-regarded captain on duty. Instead of denigrating their questions, the captain monitored by reviewing the associated medical indices (EKGs) and assured them that their diagnosis, while nonobvious, was appropriate. For the next crew, the captain made a copy of the EKGs and posted them with the following question: How would you treat this patient? A few days later, the captain posted the crew's treatment and outcome for all to see, broadcasting the unit's correct diagnosis.

RESULTS

Hypothesis Testing About Training Effectiveness

Trainees in both Exp. 1 and 2 substantially increased monitoring, positive/neutral consequences, and a type of positive consequence referred to as thanking the bearer of bad news (Table 4, Figure 1). For instance, the EMS control group acknowledged senders for pointing out prickly problems about 9% of the time it was possible to do, while those in the treatment group did it almost 20% of the time ($p = .003$).

Differences in the way in which EMS control and treatment group members responded to the same situation are shown in Tables 5, 6, and 7. When faced with a passionate diatribe about a recalcitrant group and a supposedly shoddy product, one person in the treatment group took the time to directly acknowledge the sender: "Thanks for the info." (Table 5). Responding to the same situation, another treatment group member monitored via work sampling: "Can you give me some examples, perhaps samples, of what is poor." (Table 6). In contrast, control group members often proposed directives as a solution: "If you feel the [work] is poor, I want the problem fixed," or "We should meet with Fabio to be sure he has to be more meticulous with his staff."

Differences Between Samples in Experiments 1 and 2

Although the results were more or less the same in Exp. 1 and 2, work sampling was an exception (Table 4). EMS trainees work sampled 33% of the time in comparison with merchandising trainees who did it 50% of the time ($p = .031$). This 50% figure could not be attributed to the higher level of work sampling done by the merchandising control group since essentially no differences were found between the control groups ($p = .708$).

Exploratory Probe About Antecedents

Trainees dramatically dropped their reliance on exhortations and directives as motivation when faced with problems. For example, members of the control group in the merchandising agency used antecedents alone to promote performance in roughly 13% of the situations in which it was possible, whereas the treatment group more than halved the number to approximately 5% ($p = .047$). The drop in antecedents by the treatment group in EMS was even more striking with them using far fewer in total ($p = .002$), including tacking on traditional antecedents ($p = .051$) and using them for motivation ($p = .001$).

TABLE 4 MEE Results for Treatment and Control Groups in Both Samples

CATEGORY/ Subcategory/Type	Experiment 1: Merchandising agency				Experiment 2: Emergency medical serv. (EMS)				Comparison of trtmt. groups	
	Group mean				Group mean					
	Trtmt.[c]	Contr.[d]	F	p	Trtmt.[a]	Contr.[b]	F	p	t	p
MONITORING	50.6	29.5	5.11	.047	41.7	34.4	4.38	.041	−1.4	.192
Work sample	51.8	22.1	7.39	.022	32.9	25.8	2.74	.103	−2.5	.031
Self-report	39.3	35.0	0.29	.599	37.0	32.3	1.87	.177	−0.4	.686
PROVIDING CONSEQUENCES	50.8	26.1	14.89	.003	46.7	39.7	3.82	.055	−0.7	.485
Positive/Neutral	54.0	26.5	13.75	.004	56.7	47.4	4.66	.035	0.4	.708
Simple	13.3	20.0	1.46	.255	10.8	14.6	1.01	.320	−0.6	.545
Traditional	35.2	17.7	4.24	.067	32.2	28.5	1.20	.278	0.5	.652
Thanking bearer of bad news	33.3	6.7	5.39	.043	19.8	8.6	9.47	.003	−1.4	.212
Acknowledging someone out of contact loop	5.4	0.0	1.44	.257	6.8	6.4	0.02	.898	0.3	.740
Broadcasting to multiple parties	4.8	0.0	0.69	.424	13.5	9.7	0.64	.426	1.5	.164
Letting sender/other(s) know of action	11.0	6.1	0.56	.471	9.6	10.7	0.21	.651	−0.3	.801
Relaying problem nonjudgementally	0.0	0.0	—	—	5.6	7.7	0.45	.504	2.7	.010
Negative	43.4	25.0	2.47	.147	24.1	22.4	0.12	.727	−2.3	.048

(Continued)

TABLE 4 (Continued)

CATEGORY/ Subcategory/Type	Experiment 1: Merchandising agency				Experiment 2: Emergency medical serv. (EMS)				Comparison of trtmt. groups	
	Group mean				Group mean					
	Trtmt.[c]	Contr.[d]	F	p	Trtmt.[a]	Contr.[b]	F	p	t	p
PROVIDING ANTECEDENTS	7.1	15.4	4.00	.073	16.4	26.6	10.78	.002	4.2	<.001
Tacking on traditional antecedents	8.8	17.7	1.85	.204	20.2	28.9	3.95	.051	2.7	.014
Using antecedents for motivation	5.2	12.7	5.12	.047	11.9	23.9	11.26	.001	2.4	.023

Note. Means are percentages. F values were computed from analyses of variance and t values from an independent samples t-test for equality of means, not assuming equal variances in the samples. [a] $n=32$. [b] $n=31$. [c] $n=7$. [d] $n=5$.

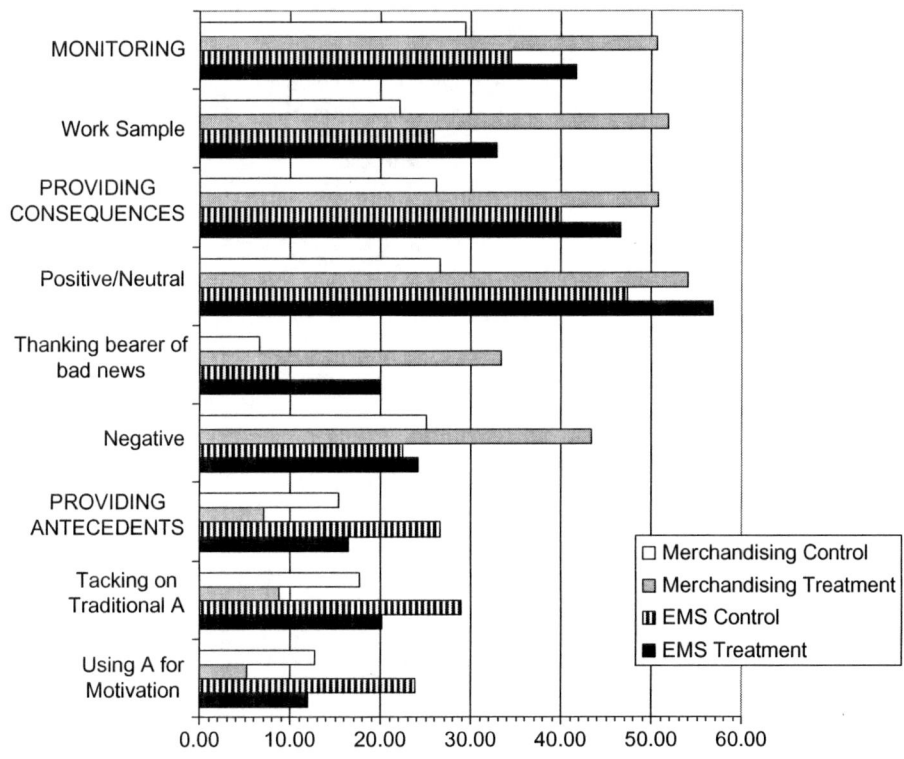

FIGURE 1 Bar chart of select categories and subcategories on the MEE for treatment and control groups in both samples. *Note.* Group means are percentage scores.

TABLE 5 Providing Positive Consequences by Thanking the Bearer of Bad News in Responses to MEE Item From EMS Treatment and Control Groups

MEE item 3 Concern expressed by employee of Dept. D about the shoddy work of Dept. E	
Responses from those in	
Treatment group	Control group
Thanks for the info. Arrange a meeting with the staff and provide examples of the . . . issues to demonstrate our concerns.	If you feel the [work] is poor, I want the problem fixed. I will e-mail the Dept. E Mgr. with your concerns.
	To Dept. E Mgr.: It has been brought to my attention from [Dept. D Employee] that [there is an issue with the work of your Dept.] Please have this problem looked into.

Note. Positive consequence is shown in italics.

TABLE 6 Monitoring via Work Sampling in Responses to MEE Item From EMS Treatment and Control Groups

MEE item 3		
Concern expressed by employee of Dept. D about the shoddy work of Dept. E		
Responses from those in		
Treatment group		Control group
Can you give me some examples, perhaps samples, of what is poor? With those in hand I can better understand the problem and more clearly relate your concerns.		We should meet with [Dept. E Dir.] to be sure he has to be more meticulous with his staff.

Note. Monitoring is shown in italics.

TABLE 7 Providing Antecedents in Responses to MEE Item From EMS Treatment and Control Groups

MEE item 1		
Complaint from employee in Dept. A about difficulty with a new form devised by Dept. B		
Responses from those in		
Treatment group		Control group
Thanks for going the extra mile to [resolve the situation]. Sorry to hear of [everyone's] frustration. I will get with the Dept. B Dir. to look at the new form and see what we can do to streamline the process.		To Dept. B Dir.: I'm told there is a problem with the [new] form. *Let's clear up the problem.*

Note. Antecedents are shown in italics.

Table 7 illustrates differences between treatment and control group members in their use of antecedents. Upon receiving news of a complaint about a new form, a treatment group member from EMS thanked the sender for working to resolve difficulties with the form, commiserated with him on his frustration, and let him know that efforts would be made to examine the form. In contrast, a member of the control group, in essence, simply relied on giving a directive ("Let's clear up the problem.").

Reactions to Training

Participants who were polled evaluated the training positively. Ninety-three percent "agreed" or "strongly agreed" on an EMS course evaluation questionnaire that they enjoyed the course and the information was useful. What they noted as the most valuable were the content ("The techniques of motivation, very helpful.") and the incorporation of examples ("Real world application to EMS situations"). Most gratifying though were comments about how the trainees felt they had been acknowledged for already doing some things well: "[The training's] given me new ideas along with what I have already implemented."

DISCUSSION

The training was effective. Seasoned managers in both the private and public sectors showed they could appropriately use the two theoretically and empirically driven behaviors of the Model in an in-basket assessment with numerous and varied simulated situations. Trainees in the treatment group provided significantly more *consequences,* particularly positive ones, even going so far as to acknowledge persons delivering bad news. One might expect that managers would recognize persons for accomplishments or even for improvements. What was particularly thrilling though was to see that trained managers did not ignore or deny the news brought to them of machines and plans gone amuck. Instead, they did just as exemplary managers in the field had done (Reynard Minnich et al., 2004), acknowledging senders bringing unsavory details to their attention: "Thanks for going the extra mile to [resolve the situation]."

More *monitors* were given as well by the treatment group in both samples. Rather than jumping to false conclusions when problems arose, trainees would more often gather information. Sometimes they would monitor via self-report: "Have you discussed the form with [Dept. B Dir.]? Is this an isolated problem or is it widespread?" Other times, they would sample the work: "Can you give me some examples, perhaps samples, of what is poor."

The most compelling result, however, was the dramatic decline in using antecedents alone as a motivational strategy. When managers learned how and why to use the Model's behaviors, directives and exhortations significantly dropped. They were less likely to rely on antecedents alone. Managers in the treatment groups used antecedent-based strategies half as often as those in control groups: a decline in the merchandising agency from 12.7% to 5.2% and in EMS from 23.9% to 11.9%. In contrast, control group managers were much more likely to try and influence others by using only antecedents. When faced with a problem, control group managers in EMS, who used them almost one quarter of the time, were likely to make assumptions without monitoring and to invoke calls for antecedents: "We have received a complaint. The client claims . . . [problems with] the service. Plz [sic] review the company policies with your employees if they need more training. . . . Plz [sic] contact [HR] to set up training times. We need to keep this client happy. Thanks!!!"

Why did the trained managers rely less on antecedents as a motivational strategy than their control group counterparts? Were antecedents disparaged during training? Were trainees told to refrain from using antecedents? Were consequences and monitors held up as being far superior to antecedents? No, no, and no. In fact, the training barely mentioned antecedents.[8] One explanation is that monitoring and providing consequences, when presented in context with evidence and practice and feedback, are palpable and convincing as motivational strategies. And given a viable alternative, managers did not need to revert to traditional antecedent strategies.

The opportunity to try using the behaviors of the Model on the job and then return the next week to report on their efforts to an avid audience of their peers was a highlight of the training at the merchandising agency. For instance, one trainee jubilantly reported how after opening a box of merchandise and checking on the packaging, he immediately noticed how the packaging lent itself to breakage and how he was able to make modifications, enabling him to drop the package from a second-story landing without a hitch. He attributed this timely monitor via work sampling to saving him from a potentially distraught client. Although both samples increased their monitoring, positive/neutral consequences, and thanking the bearer of bad news, it was interesting to note that the merchandising trainees who applied the concepts on the job actually provided more work samples than the control group and the EMS trainees. Perhaps it is necessary to build in practice on the job and provide feedback to ensure that managers can really learn how to incorporate monitor via work sampling, just as exemplary managers have done, into their daily management routines.

The in-basket assessment, a relative newcomer to training evaluation, proved noteworthy in its ability to convey the nuance and passion with which managers managed in a variety of situations. The 21 true-to-life scenarios ranged from standard reports to vociferous complaints about pressing issues. Furthermore, each respondent reacted to the same set of incidents, thus enabling a true comparison between treatment and control groups. At the same time, respondents could reply to whomever they wished in their own words. Hence, one could see how trained managers adroitly embraced the concepts and succinctly provided positive consequences and monitored ("Just looked at numbers for the last four years. Great job! Especially last year. What did you do differently that resulted in such a large gain in the last year?"). Lastly, the MEE provides a viable alternative to observations, which although often rich, sensitive, and reliable, are sometimes logistically difficult to do and hence limited to certain situations.

---

[8] With the exception of a brief mention in Exp. 1 at the end of week 4 about avoiding antecedents when providing a negative consequence.

In sum, seasoned managers can learn during a relatively short period how to successfully motivate others. These results were replicated with seasoned managers in two different settings in the private and public sectors. Perhaps best of all, learning these behaviors has the effect of reducing otherwise lackluster but prevalent strategies involving antecedents.

REFERENCES

Barling, J., Weber, T., & Kelloway, E. K. (1996). Effects of transformational leadership training on attitudinal and financial outcomes: A field experiment. *Journal of Applied Psychology, 81*, 827–832. doi:10.1037/0021-9010.81.6.827

Bass, B. M. (1985). Leadership: Good, better, best. *Organizational Dynamics, 13*, 26–40. doi:10.1016/0090-2616(85)90028-2

Campbell, J. P., Dunnette, M. D., Lawler, E. E., & Weick, K. E. (1970). *Managerial behavior, performance, and effectiveness.* New York, NY: McGraw-Hill.

Daniels, A. C. (2000). *Bringing out the best in people: How to apply the astonishing power of positive reinforcement* (2nd ed.). New York, NY: McGraw-Hill.

Deci, E. L., Connell, J. P., & Ryan, R. M. (1989). Self-determination in a work organization. *Journal of Applied Psychology, 74*, 580–590. doi:10.1037/0021-9010.74.4.580

Dorfman, P. W., Stephan, W. G., & Loveland, J. (1986). Performance appraisal behaviors: Supervisor perceptions and subordinate reactions. *Personnel Psychology, 39*, 579–597. doi:10.1111/j.1744-6570.1986.tb00954.x

Dvir, T., Eden, D., Avolio, B. J., & Shamir, B. (2002). Impact of transformational leadership on follower development and performance: A field experiment. *Academy of Management Journal, 45*, 735–744. doi:10.2307/3069307

Fleishman, E. A. (1973). Twenty years of consideration and structure. In E. A. Fleishman & J. G. Hunt (Eds.), *Current developments in the study of leadership* (pp. 1–37). Carbondale, IL: Southern Illinois University Press.

Graen, G. B., Novak, M. A., & Sommerkamp, P. (1982). The effects of leader-member exchange and job design on productivity and satisfaction: Testing a dual attachment model. *Organizational Behavior and Human Performance, 30*, 109–131. doi:10.1016/0030-5073(82)90236-7

House, R. J. (1977). A 1976 theory of charismatic leadership. In J. G. Hunt & L. L. Larson (Eds.), *Leadership: The cutting edge* (pp. 189–207). Carbondale, IL: Southern Illinois University Press.

Johnson, G. A. (1975). The relative efficacy of stimulus versus reinforcement control for obtaining stable performance change. *Organizational Behavior and Human Performance, 14*, 321–341.

Komaki, J. L. (1998). *Leadership from an operant perspective.* London, England: Routledge.

Komaki, J., Heinzmann, A. T., & Lawson, L. (1980). Effect of training and feedback: Component analysis of a behavioral safety program. *Journal of Applied Psychology, 65*, 261–270. doi:10.1037//0021-9010.65.3.261

Komaki, J. L., Newlin, M. H., & Desselles, M. L. (1990, April). Walking on the wild side: Criterion related validation of an in-basket exercise of supervisory behaviors. In M. H. Newlin (Chair), *Simulated performance assessment: Fact or fantasy?* Symposium conducted at the conference of the Society of Industrial and Organizational Psychology, Miami, FL.

Lawrence, H. V., & Wiswell, A. K. (1993). Using the work group as a laboratory for learning: Increasing leadership and team effectiveness through feedback. *Human Resource Development Quarterly, 4*, 135–148. doi:10.1016/0030-5073(82)90236-7

Locke, E. A., & Latham, G. P. (1990). *A theory of goal setting and task performance.* Englewood Cliffs, NJ: Prentice Hall.

Mager, R. F., & Pipe, P. (1984). *Analyzing performance problems* (2nd ed.). Belmont, CA: Pitman.

May, G. L., & Kahnweiler, W. M. (2000). The effect of a mastery practice design on learning and transfer in behavior modeling training. *Personnel Psychology, 53*, 353–373.

Methot, L. L., Williams, W. L., Cummings, A., & Bradshaw, B. (1996). Measuring the effects of a manager-supervisor training program through the generalized performance of managers, supervisors, front-line staff and clients in a human service setting. *Journal of Organizational Behavior Management, 16*(2), 3–34. doi:10.1300/J075v16n02_02

Miller, L. K. (1997). *Principles of everyday behavior analysis* (3rd ed.). Belmont, CA: Wadsworth.

Paquet, B., Kasl, E., Weinstein, L., & Waite, W. (1987). The bottom line. *Training & Development Journal, 41*, 27–33.

Patel, L. (2010). 2010 State of the industry: Continued dedication to workplace learning. *T+D, 64*(11), 48–53.

Reynard Minnich, M., Komaki, J. L., & Donovan, C. (2004, April). Predicting supervisory effectiveness using an in-basket assessment suitable for selection. Poster presented at the Conference of the Society for Industrial and Organizational Psychology, Chicago, IL.

Russell, J. S., Wexley, K. N., & Hunter, J. E. (1984). Questioning the effectiveness of behavior modeling training in an industrial setting. *Personnel Psychology, 37*, 465–481. doi:10.1111/j.1744-6570.1984.tb00523.x

Salas, E. (2010, December). *The science and practice of teamwork: A quarter century of progress.* Symposium conducted at the meeting of the Metropolitan New York Association of Applied Psychology, New York, NY.

Salas, E., & Cannon-Bowers, J. A. (2001). The science of training: A decade of progress. *Annual Review of Psychology, 52*, 471–499. doi:10.1146/annurev.psych.52.1.471

Salas, E., Milham, L. M., & Bowers, C. A. (2003). Training evaluation in the military: Misconceptions, opportunities, and challenges. *Military Psychology, 15*, 3–16. doi:10.1207/S15327876MP1501_01

Sayles, L. (1979). *Leadership: What effective managers really do…and how they do it.* New York, NY: McGraw-Hill.

Scandura, T. A., & Graen, G. B. (1984). Moderating effects of initial leader-member exchange status on the effects of a leadership intervention. *Journal of Applied Psychology, 69*, 428–436. doi:10.1037//0021-9010.69.3.428

Schippmann, J. S., Prien, E. P., & Katz, J. A. (1990). Reliability and validity of in-basket performance measures. *Personnel Psychology, 43*, 837–859. doi:10.1111/j.1744-6570.1990.tb00685.x

Smith, R. M., White, P. E., & Montello, P. A. (1992). Investigation of interpersonal management training for educational administrators. *Journal of Educational Research, 85*, 242–245.

Steers, R. M., & Porter, L. W. (Eds.). (1990). *Motivation and work behavior* (5th ed.). New York, NY: McGraw-Hill.

Tracey, J. B., Tannenbaum, S. I., & Kavanagh, M. J. (1995). Applying trained skills on the job: The importance of the work environment. *Journal of Applied Psychology, 80*, 239–252. doi:10.1037//0021-9010.80.2.239

Wexley, K. N. (1984). Personnel training. *Annual Review of Psychology, 35*, 519–551.

Managing Performance to Change Behavior

ANGELO S. DeNISI
Tulane University, New Orleans, Louisiana, USA

Performance appraisal systems are often considered primarily in their role as criterion measures for validation studies. Even when they are considered in other organizational roles, there has traditionally been a strong focus on improving the accuracy of the appraisals. The present article argues that the proper focus of performance appraisal is to change employees' behavior on the job—both task performance behavior and contextual performance. Specifically, appraisals are best considered as part of a larger performance management system, where the entire focus is on improving performance. Such a focus has important implications for how concerned we are about perceived accuracy and fairness. Furthermore, when viewed in this way, it is clear that we must consider how to leverage individual level performance up to the level of the firm, since improving firm performance is critical to any organization's strategic goals.

Performance appraisals, in some form, are conducted in almost every organization. Typically, appraisals are an annual event involving preparation on the part of both the employee (the ratee) and the rater (often a supervisor), followed by the rater's assignment of "scores" on some aspects of the ratee's performance, and ending with the two parties sitting together to discuss the appraisal and make plans for the future. Traditionally, both parties are somewhat dissatisfied with the process and its outcomes (see, for example, Meyer, Kay, & French, 1965; Pulakos, 2004), and there have been almost one hundred years worth of studies that have identified problems with the rating forms used (e.g., Thorndike, 1920), the aspects of performance included (e.g., Flanagan, 1954), as well as with the actual performance review at the end (e.g., Landy, Barnes, & Murphy, 1978). As a result, there have been calls to cease conducting performance appraisals and replace them with some other form of evaluation (e.g., Coens & Jenkins, 2000), yet performance appraisals are still done in most organizations. Why?

There are actually a number of reasons why performance appraisals endure. Performance appraisals still serve as a primary mechanism for providing feedback, and information from performance appraisals remains a major source of input for important human resource decisions. However, even though these reasons are important, in order to understand why performance appraisals remain a central piece of any human resource management system, it is important to understand that appraisals represent only one part of a more important process—the performance management process. It is even more important to understand that the performance management process is absolutely critical to any enterprise, and that it is focused primarily upon changing behavior at work. The major goals of this article are to discuss why performance management is so important for behavior change and to discuss relevant aspects of the performance management process. But first, it is important to set the stage by discussing some of the stated reasons why organizations conduct appraisals.

PURPOSES FOR PERFORMANCE APPRAISAL

A number of authors have discussed various reasons why organizations conduct appraisals, and several have even proposed models. For example, Cleveland, Murphy, and Williams (1989) discussed purposes for appraisals that fell into four categories: between person decisions (e.g., promotion and salary decisions); within person decisions (e.g., feedback and identifying training needs); systems maintenance (e.g., manpower planning and evaluation of HR systems); and documentation (e.g., criteria for validity studies and meeting legal needs). This classification system is more complex than earlier discussions of the primary purposes for conducting appraisals, and it also emphasizes the multiple uses of appraisal information in companies.

Furthermore, there is evidence to suggest that the perceived purpose of appraisals can affect how raters process information and even the ratings they assign. For example, studies have shown that inflation of ratings is more likely to occur when appraisals are used for decision making (cf. Murphy & Cleveland, 1995; Chapter 4), and the difference between private judgments and public ratings varied as a function of the purpose for the appraisal (cf. Murphy & Cleveland, 1995). Furthermore, Williams, DeNisi, Blencoe, and Cafferty (1985) found that appraisal purpose determined what kinds of information a rater searched for and how that information was stored in memory, which affects the actual appraisal decisions made.

Among Industrial/Organizational (I/O) psychologists and those interested in organizational behavior management (OBM), however, most of the interest in performance appraisal has been in its role as a criterion variable. In the case of I/O psychologists, much of the focus has been on using appraisals as criteria in validation studies. That is, the operational definition of proving a selection technique is "job related" involves demonstrating that scores on the test are related to some measure of performance on the job. Dunnette (1963) was instrumental in arguing that low validity coefficients were often obtained because of faulty criterion measures. Specifically, he cited problems with the reliability (and accuracy) or the performance ratings that were typically used as criterion measures. Scholars in the OBM area were interested in defining effective performance so they could target behaviors to be changed and determine whether any such attempts to change behavior were effective (cf. Komaki & Minnich, 2001).

But it has been the I/O perspective that has had the greatest impact on performance appraisal research, and this perspective has primarily resulted in efforts to improve the accuracy of performance appraisals by developing better rating scales or by training raters. Unfortunately, assessments of rating accuracy require some standard or "true score" against which to compare the ratings obtained, and such true scores are difficult (if not impossible) to obtain in the field. As a result, scholars and practitioners came to rely upon proxies for accuracy—especially proxies related to rating errors—such that reduced rating errors were assumed to indicate increased accuracy. This assumption, as it turned out, was wrong. First of all, traditional rating "errors" such as leniency or halo, may not be errors at all, but instead, may simply reflect response tendencies (cf. Bernardin & Pence, 1980; DeNisi & Peters, 1996). Furthermore, there are data to suggest that increased errors (especially halo "error") may be actually associated with increased accuracy (Murphy & Balzer, 1989).

By the time these issues became clear, however, there was already a body of research devoted to developing better rating scales that could increase accuracy—operationalized as the decrease of either rating errors or rater disagreements. These studies produced recommendations for new scale formats such as Forced Distribution Rating Scales (Berkshire & Highland, 1953), or Behaviorally Anchored Rating Scales (e.g., Smith & Kendall, 1963), as well as for the design or training raters to reduce rating errors in their evaluations (e.g., Latham, Wexley, & Pursell, 1975). This type of research, though, decreased dramatically with the publication of a landmark review paper by Landy and Farr (1980), which concluded that there was no evidence that any one rating scale was consistently better than any other scale.

The recognition that changing the rating scale might not affect rating accuracy also shifted the focus of research efforts to rater cognitive processes that might be more closely related to rating accuracy. Several models were proposed and discussed (e.g., Feldman, 1981; Ilgen & Feldman, 1983; DeNisi, Cafferty, & Meglino, 1984). The studies that followed were almost exclusively laboratory studies (although see DeNisi & Peters [1996] and Varma, DeNisi, & Peters [1996] for exceptions), and used rating accuracy as a dependent variable. In fact, many of the cognitive processes that were studied were found to be related to rating accuracy (see review in DeNisi, 1996), but these efforts also led to concerns over better ways to assess accuracy. In fact, most of the "cognitive" studies were conducted in laboratory settings where it is possible to construct "true scores." Borman (1977) pioneered the use of videotapes that portrayed known levels of performance that allowed for the direct assessment of accuracy (although there have been disagreements about the best formula for computing accuracy; cf. Sulsky & Balzer, 1988). Furthermore, scholars and practitioners began considering interventions that could improve accuracy directly, such as "frame of reference" training (Bernardin & Buckley, 1981; Pulakos, 1984). But things were about to change again.

SO, WHAT DO WE WANT INSTEAD?

Those changes came with the publication of papers (e.g., Ilgen, 1993; DeNisi & Gonzalez, 2004) arguing that, even if we could assess and improve rating accuracy, this was the wrong criterion measure. That is not to say that rating accuracy is a "bad" thing. All things equal, it is better to have accurate than inaccurate ratings (cf. DeNisi & Sonesh, 2011). Of course, rating accuracy *is* important for those who are interested in performance appraisals primarily as criterion measures for validation studies. But, in addition, accurate ratings are more likely to be perceived by employees as fairer, and individuals are more likely to respond positively to feedback they believe to be accurate (cf. Ilgen, Fisher, & Taylor, 1979). The problem comes when improved accuracy, in and of itself, becomes the final criterion by which appraisal systems are judged. For example, Cardy and Dobbins (1994) discuss a myriad of accuracy measures, along with their advantages and disadvantage of each, but despite technical merits of an index such as stereotype accuracy, such a measure may have little meaning to a person being rated. As a result, improved stereotype accuracy is less likely to be perceived as important by an employee and so will be less likely to motivate employees to change behavior—yet that is exactly what we need to have happen.

Ultimately, what we want is for employees to change their behavior in ways that lead to improved performance. In order for this to occur, employees must see a need for behavior change, be able to change their behavior, and then see how that change will be associated with positive outcomes. But the first step is for the employee to believe and accept the feedback that he or she receives. Thus, it is critical to go beyond mere concerns with accuracy and focus instead on how appraisals can be used to change behavior and improve performance. Fortunately, this is exactly the view that scholars and practitioners began to adopt. If we examine the purposes discussed above, from Cleveland et al. (1989), we can see that many of these purposes can be reduced to demonstrating to an employee where he or she needed improvement (i.e., strengths and weaknesses), and then showing the employee that valued outcomes were associated with improvement. That is, most of the emphasis is on getting employees to change their behavior in order to improve their performance on the job, which lies at the heart of the arguments by Ilgen (1993), and DeNisi and Gonzalez (2004).

But in order for employees to respond to feedback about their performance in the desired manner, they must believe that they deserve the rating they received. As noted above, all things equal, more accurate ratings should produce stronger perceptions that these ratings are fair, but the important thing is the perception of fairness. Research on organizational justice has been especially useful in helping us to understand the importance of these perceptions. For example, in the case of distributive justice (e.g., Greenberg, 1986), the employee must feel that his or her inputs were recognized in the same way as another employee's inputs. If the employee feels that she or he hasn't received the rating that was deserved, the employee will most likely reject the feedback and not bother to change behavior. Note that it doesn't matter whether the employee's perception is correct or not—it is the perception itself that matters.

But it is also important for the employee to perceive that the process used to determine the ratings was fair. This consideration of "procedural justice" is probably more important than distributive justice. It is important that the processes involved be transparent, and it is useful if the employee has some voice in the process, or some possibility of appeal. This is the disadvantage of trying to improve rating accuracy by using complex formulae for determining accuracy. For most employees, the simpler the process, the more transparent it is, and the more likely it is to be perceived as fair. In fact, several studies (e.g., Johnson, 2005; Taylor, Tracy, Renard, Harrison, & Carroll, 1995) have demonstrated that employee reactions are more positive, and behavior change is more likely when employees perceive the ratings and evaluation procedures as fair.

This discussion leads to the conclusion that, in order for performance feedback to be effective, it must be accepted and, eventually, acted upon. The discussion of issues of fairness and justice are surely relevant to any consideration of feedback acceptance, but it is also important to note that the level of effectiveness of feedback may not be as high as many people believe. Kluger and DeNisi (1996) conducted a historical review and meta-analysis of the effects of individual feedback on subsequent performance. They found that, in roughly a third of the cases considered, feedback had a negative effect on subsequent performance. That is, individuals receiving feedback performed more poorly subsequent to receiving feedback than did individuals receiving no feedback—regardless of the sign of the feedback.

The important aspect of this article, for the present discussion, is that Kluger and DeNisi (1996) found that the aspects of feedback usually associated with feedback acceptance, such as the source of the feedback (e.g., Herold, Liden, & Leatherwood, 1987), or the sign of the feedback (e.g., Ilgen et al., 1979) were not as important as had been believed, and that the role feedback played on subsequent behavior was much more complex than had been understood. Yet, it was still clear that, if individuals failed to accept feedback, regardless of the reason, they would not be likely to change their behavior (cf. Ilgen et al., 1979; Kluger & DeNisi, 1996, 1998). Thus, if appraisals and feedback are intended to help employees improve their job performance, the employee must accept the feedback, feel able to improve their performance as desired, and see some reason for exerting the effort to change their behavior. That is why it would seem more worthwhile to consider models of motivation rather than just measurement, and to expand our view to include performance management rather than just performance appraisal.

Before turning to performance management and behavior change, it is worth considering exactly what type of performance we are interested in influencing. Specifically, it is worth considering the role of contextual performance in this setting, as opposed to task performance. The term contextual performance was first used by Borman and Motowidlo (1993), and refers to something closely related to the concept of Organizational Citizenship Behavior (OCB; Organ, 1988). Task performance refers to performance of those tasks and behaviors that are specified by a job description, and these behaviors are the proper focus of performance appraisals. Contextual performance, then, refers to behavior that is not specified by any job description; that is generally beneficial to the organization; but is not required by anyone in a formal way. The behaviors involved run the gamut from helping coworkers, to volunteering for overtime, and defending the company to outsiders (cf. Borman, 2004).

It would clearly be useful if we could increase the frequency with which these behaviors occur as well, but how to do this is not obvious. Some scholars have suggested that there are critical personality variables that determine who engages in these behaviors (e.g., Borman, Penner, Allen, & Motowidlo, 2001), which would make this more of a selection problem than a performance management problem. Others have argued that contextual performance is simply another form of impression management (e.g., Bolino, Varela, Bande, & Turnely, 2006), but many others argue that employees engage in these behaviors in return for good treatment by the organization (see review by Brief & Motowidlo, 1986). Since OCBs or contextual performance behaviors are not required of anyone, they cannot (by definition) become part of the formal appraisal process and so cannot easily be rewarded, but they might be encouraged by simply treating employees with respect.

Interestingly, several scholars have found that contextual performance does influence appraisal decisions—even decisions regarding task performance, and so this behavior can be, and is, rewarded (e.g., Van Scotter, Motowidlo, & Cross, 2000). One can argue about the fairness of evaluating an employee on the basis of behaviors that are not required on the job, but Borman (1987) found that army officers believed this willingness to go above and beyond was one of the most important determinants of subordinate effectiveness. In any case, I would suggest that any attempt to change behavior by managing performance should consider both task performance and contextual performance, especially if we want to improve firm-level performance.

Finally, as noted earlier, behavioral (e.g., OBM) scholars have always been interested in studying behavioral change and so have always understood the link between the measurement of performance and the changing of behavior. Weitz (1961) was one of the first to introduce the idea of criteria for evaluating criterion measures, but his notion was expanded upon by authors such as Komaki and her colleagues (Komaki, 1998; Komaki & Minnich, 2001). Since these authors were most interested in ways of assessing behavioral change, they argued using the "wrong" performance measure could either obscure any changes that had occurred or might lead one to believe that change had occurred when this was not actually the case.

Komaki (1998) went even further arguing for what she termed the SURF & C criteria. Her point was that, if we used the "wrong" criterion measures, efforts to motivate employees to change their behavior would not be effective, and so it was important that we target behaviors and use criterion measures (such as performance appraisals) that focused on behaviors that were directly sampled rather than obtained from secondary sources (S), under the control of the person being evaluated (U), reliable in terms of interrater agreement (R), assessed frequently (F), and critical for the successful completion of the job (C). These suggestions have not been explicitly included in the discussion of most performance management models, but they are consistent with motivational approaches to performance appraisals and the resultant models of performance management that we now discuss.

. . . AND SO, MOTIVATIONAL MODELS AND PERFORMANCE MANAGEMENT

If the goal of appraisal is ultimately to change and improve performance, then the key is certainly performance management. Performance management refers to the variety of activities, initiated by the supervisor, to influence the behavior of the subordinate (cf. Aguinis, 2009). These activities often include providing feedback, setting goals for future performance, and providing incentives tied to improved performance. Also, while performance appraisals typically occur once or twice a year, performance management is an ongoing process of intervention. In the final analysis, then, the details of any performance appraisal system may not be as important as the details of the corresponding performance management system. The two are, of course related (if managers focus on and reward the "wrong" behaviors, no system of performance management will be successful), but the critical part of the process is what we do with the appraisal information we collect. This is why it is so important to integrate models of motivation into the performance management process—the key to success is to persuade employees to improve their performance on the job, and that involves motivation.

Insights from goal-setting and expectancy theory are both useful for informing performance management systems. Surely one of the most important aspects of any performance management system is the setting of goals. Goal-setting is well-established as a motivational tool in the literature (cf. Locke & Latham, 1990), but as part of the performance management process, goal setting needs to be tied to strategic planning. That is, the process must begin with what a firm is trying to accomplish. These strategic goals must then be translated down to the level of an individual employee or group of employees, but it is critical that, if the employee (or group of employees) accomplish their goals, this must help the firm accomplish its strategic goals (I will return to this idea later when discussing firm-level performance). If an employee can accomplish his or her goals but that makes the firm no closer to accomplishing its goals, then the employee has the wrong goals. Therefore, the identification of the right goals and how they will be assessed must be part of the performance management system (cf. Pulakos, 2009).

Once these goals are set, it is important that the employee receive regular feedback concerning progress toward goal attainment. Regular feedback is a part of all performance management systems, but it is important to ensure that the feedback is having the desired effect on employee effort because, as noted earlier, the effects of feedback on performance may be more complex than had been believed (cf. Kluger & DeNisi, 1996, 1998). Although the present article cannot do justice to the various aspects of feedback that must be considered, it is important to realize that an evaluation of feedback effectiveness is critical.

Of course, it is also critical that there are rewards or some positive outcomes associated with accomplishing goals, and this is where expectancy-type models are useful. Employees must see that the accomplishment of goals will increase the chances that they receive money, promotions, or some other type of outcome. The stronger the connection between goal accomplishment and the reception of valued outcomes, the stronger the motivation to work to accomplish goals. This is also the basic notion behind any expectancy-type model of motivation, and the interested reader is referred especially to Naylor, Pritchard, and Ilgen (1980) for a rather complete and rich version of an expectancy model. This model is also the basis for the Productivity Measurement and Enhancement System (ProMES; Pritchard, Jones, Roth, Steubing, & Ekeberg, 1988), an integrated system for improving productivity at work, which has been found to be extremely effective in the United States as well as the rest of the world (Pritchard, Holling, Lammers, & Clark, 2002).

It is the effective combination of feedback, goals, and rewards that is most likely to influence employees to change their behavior in ways that result in improved performance. As noted earlier, employees must perceive the feedback (i.e., the evaluations) they receive as fair, but they must then be helped to develop goals and strategies to improve their performance. They are much more likely to engage in these processes if they can clearly see how performance improvement will result in their obtaining valued rewards and outcomes, and DeNisi and Pritchard (2006) developed a performance management model based on these principles.

MORE THAN INDIVIDUAL PERFORMANCE

The discussion of ProMES also raises questions about performance improvement at levels of analysis beyond that of the individual. I have stated that a critical goal of performance management is to improve performance, but most of the discussion thus far has been focused on individual performance only. In fact, organizations are interested in improving individual performance only to the extent that it results in an improvement in firm performance (although a discussion of the various measures of firm performance is well beyond the scope of this article). We know quite a bit about how to change individual behavior, but assuming we can change the behavior of individual, how can we move to improved performance at the organizational level?

Many approaches and models of performance management focus almost entirely upon individual level performance, and so seem to imply that if we use performance management tools to improve individual level performance and to develop critical competencies, firm level performance will improve as well (cf. Aguinis, 2009; Pulakos, 2004, 2009). There are certainly situations where this would be the case. For example, if every bowler on a bowling team improves his or her score, the team's score will improve exactly by the same degree. But, if every teller in a bank improved his or her performance, would the bank's financial performance also improve? Would its stock price rise? Perhaps so, but those corporate level performance measures clearly go far beyond a simple compilation of the individual performance ratings of the tellers. Furthermore, although research on appraising and rewarding team performance (e.g., Brannick, Salas, & Prince, 1997;

Smither, 1998) provides useful ideas, it does little to help us move up to improving firm-level performance.

There have been suggestions, however, for ways to manage the performance of teams. This is, at least, performance at a level of analysis higher than that of the individual employee, but as I shall discuss, this is probably not the solution to the larger problem. In any case, the relationship between individual and team level performance is also complex, and it depends upon such factors as the nature of the technology (e.g., Goodman, 1986) and the nature of the task (e.g., Saavedra, Earley, & Van Dyne, 1993). But whereas all of these factors are important, the most critical for the link between individual and team-level performance is probably the nature of the task, since this imposes boundary conditions on the strength and nature of that relationship.

In the simplest case, team performance is nothing more than the aggregate of the performance of individuals (cf. Kozlowski, Gully, Nason, & Smith, 1999). This is the case in Ryder Cup competition in golf or Davis Cup competition in tennis, where the performance of one individual is independent from the performance of any other individual. It is more typical, though, to have a situation where the performance of one team member is dependent (at least in part) upon the performance of other team members. For example, the performance of the quarterback on a football team depends in part upon the performance of the members of the offensive line as well as the performance of running backs and receivers. In these cases, intangibles such as "teamwork" or "backing-up behavior" (e.g., Porter, 2005) become more critical, but are much more difficult to assess. Therefore, in these cases we typically rely upon measures of team performance only and largely ignore individual performance. This can result in free-riding or social loafing (e.g., Latane, Williams, & Harkins, 1979), where individuals feel they can reduce their efforts because the slack will be taken up by other team members (although this is unlikely in professional sports' teams).

Therefore, managing team performance can provide some insights into the issues involved in managing performance at the firm level, but issues remain. In any case, as noted by DeNisi (2000), one of the critical issues in moving from individual level to firm-level performance is ensuring that performance must be managed at the desired level of behavior change. But this is not such a simple matter. Even though it may be possible to reward all team members for behaviors that result in improved team performance, it is more difficult to reward all employees for behavior that results in improved firm-level performance—but it is not impossible. Several years ago, Continental Airlines wanted to improve its' "on-time departure" scores. The company announced that every month that Continental was listed among the top three for on-time departures, each employee would receive a bonus of a stated amount. Furthermore, any month that Continental was listed as the best airline for on time departures, every employee would receive an additional bonus. It was clear to see how employees exerted extra effort to make sure the passengers got on the plane and seated so a flight could leave on schedule.

But this example is the exception rather than the rule for firm-level performance. It was easy for the airline employees to see how their behavior would influence the score for on-time departures, but bank tellers probably cannot see how their behavior influences a bank's balance sheet—especially if those balance sheets are hampered with bad loans made by someone else. This concept is usually referred to as the "line of sight problem" (e.g., Boswell & Boudreau, 2001). Quite simply, it suggests that if employees can see how their behavior affects performance at a higher level, it is easier to change their behavior in such a way that firm performance increases as well. When there is no "line of sight" for the employee, however, rewards based on firm-level performance are unlikely to influence employee behavior.

It is worth noting that, although there has been an increasing interest in the relationship between HR practices and firm performance in recent years (e.g., Huselid, 1996), little is known about exactly *how* these practices can influence firm-level performance. There seems to be an assumption that if a firm hires the best people, trains them, and rewards them properly, the firm will do better. But this ignores problems such as firms enacting the "wrong" strategy, or executives making other poor decisions that hurt the firm's performance. Furthermore, such an assumption suggests "bottom-up" approaches (cf. Kozlowski et al., 1999), where performance improvements at lower levels influence performance at higher subsequent levels, all the way up to the firm level. Performance management systems, on the other hand, are technically "top down" approaches, since they begin with firm-level goals and then use these to help set goals at the next lowest level and so on down, but both make similar assumptions about how individual performance is related to firm-level performance. Perhaps future research—where I/O Psychology and OBM scholars, who know about behavioral change, could work with strategy scholars who know about firm-level performance—might show us how to translate individual performance improvements into improvements at the firm level as well.

CONCLUSIONS

An important reason for organizations to conduct performance appraisals is to improve performance at work. Thus, the proper focus of much of our attention to appraisals should be on how to use them to change behavior. Although OBM scholars have been more attuned to this need than others, it is nonetheless the case that a great deal of research in this area has been focused on ways of making appraisals more accurate, rather than more effective in changing behavior. As a result, improving appraisal systems has been viewed as a measurement problem rather than a motivation problem. Instead, I have argued that we need to focus on the larger process of performance management—which is concerned with changing behavior—rather than on the more narrow process of performance appraisal.

Recent shifts in emphasis toward performance management have begun to produce research aimed at ways of changing behavior and improving performance, at least at the individual level. But, in the end, we must find ways to leverage individual performance—both task performance and contextual performance—improvements up to the level of firm performance.

REFERENCES

Aguinis, H. (2009). *Performance management* (2nd ed.). Upper Saddle River, NJ: Pearson/Prentice Hall.

Berkshire, H., & Highland, R. (1953). Forced-choice performance rating: A methodological stud. *Personnel Psychology, 6*, 355–378.

Bernardin, H. J., & Buckley, M. R. (1981). A consideration of strategies in rater training. *Academy of Management, 6*, 205–212.

Bernardin, H. J., & Pence, E. C. (1980). Effects of rater training: Creating new response sets and decreasing accuracy. *Journal of Applied Psychology, 65*, 60–66.

Bolino, M. C., Varela, J. A., Bande, B., & Turnely, W. H. (2006). The impact of impression management tactics on supervisor ratings of organizational citizenship behaviors. *Journal of Organizational Behavior, 27*, 281–297.

Borman, W. C. (1977). Consistency of rating accuracy and rater errors in the judgment of human performance. *Organizational Behavior and Human Decision Processes, 20*, 238–252.

Borman, W. C. (1987). Personal constructs, performance schemata, and "folk theories" of subordinate effectiveness: Exploration in an army officer sample. *Organizational Behavior and Human Decision Processes, 40*, 307–322.

Borman, W. C. (2004). The concept of organizational citizenship. *Current Directions in Psychological Science, 13*, 238–241.

Borman, W. C., Penner, L. A., Allen, T. D., & Motowidlo, S. J. (2001). Personality predictors of citizenship performance. *International Journal of Selection and Assessment, 9*, 52–69.

Borman, W. C., & Motowidlo, S. J. (1993). Expanding the criterion domain to include elements of contextual performance. In N. Schmitt & W. Borman (Eds.), *Personnel selection in organizations* (pp.71–98). San Francisco, CA: Jossey-Bass.

Boswell, W. R., & Boudreau, J. W. (2001). How leading companies create, measure, and achieve results through "line of sight." *Management Decisions, 39*, 851–859.

Brannick, M. T., Salas, E., & Prince, C. (Eds.). (1997). *Team performance assessment and measurement: Theory, methods, and applications.* Mahwah, NJ: Erlbaum.

Brief, A. P., & Motowidlo, S. J. (1986). Prosocial organizational behavior. *Academy of Management Review, 11*, 710–725.

Cardy, R. L., & Dobbins, G. H. (1994). *Performance appraisal: Alternative perspectives*. Cincinnati, OH: South-Western Publishing.

Cleveland, J. N., Murphy, K. R., & Williams, R. E. (1989). Multiple uses of performance appraisal: Prevalence and correlates. *Journal of Applied Psychology, 74*, 130–135.

Coens, T., & Jenkins, M. (2000). *Abolishing performance appraisals: Why they backfire and what to do instead*. San Francisco, CA: Berrett-Keohler.

DeNisi, A. S. (1996). *Cognitive processes in performance appraisal: A research agenda with implications for practice*. London, England: Routledge.

DeNisi, A. S. (2000). Performance appraisal and control systems: A Multilevel approach. In K. Klein & S. Kozlowski (Eds.), *Multilevel theory, research, and methods in organizations* (pp. 121–156). San Francisco, CA: SIOP Frontiers Series, Jossey-Bass.

DeNisi, A. S., Cafferty, T. P., & Meglino, B. M. (1984). A cognitive view of the performance appraisal process: A model and research propositions. *Organizational Behavior and Human Performance, 33*, 360–396.

DeNisi, A. S., & Gonzalez, J. A. (2004). Design performance appraisal to improve performance. In E. A. Locke (Ed.), *The Blackwell handbook of principles of organizational behavior* (pp. 60–72). London, England: Blackwell.

DeNisi, A. S., & Peters, L. H. (1996). The organization of information in memory and the performance appraisal process: Evidence from the field. *Journal of Applied Psychology, 81*, 717–737.

DeNisi, A. S., & Pritchard, R. D. (2006). Improving individual performance: A motivational framework. *Management and Organization Review, 2*, 253–277.

DeNisi, A. S., & Sonesh, S. (2011). Appraising and managing performance at work. In S. Zedeck, H. Aquinis, & J. Zhou (Eds.), *Handbook of industrial and organizational psychology* (pp. 255–280). Washington, DC: American Psychological Association.

Dunnette, M. D. (1963). A note on the criterion. *Journal of Applied Psychology, 47*, 351–354.

Feldman, J. M. (1981). Beyond attribution theory: Cognitive processes in performance appraisal. *Journal of Applied Psychology, 66*, 127–148.

Flanagan, J. C. (1954). The critical incident technique. *Psychological Bulletin, 51*, 327–358.

Goodman, P. S. (1986). Impact of task and technology on group performance. In P. S. Goodman (Ed.), *Designing effective work groups* (pp. 120–167). San Francisco, CA: Jossey-Bass.

Greenberg, J. (1986). Determinants of perceived fairness of performance evaluations. *Journal of Applied Psychology, 71*, 340–342.

Herold, D. M., Liden, R. C., & Leatherwood, M. L. (1987). Using multiple attributes to assess sources of performance feedback. *Academy of Management Journal, 30*, 826–835.

Huselid, M. A. (1996). The impact of human resource management practices on turnover, productivity, and corporate financial reporting. *Academy of Management Journal, 39*, 779–801.

Ilgen, D. R. (1993). Performance appraisal accuracy: An illusive and sometimes misguided goal. In H. Schuler, J. L. Farr, & M. Smith (Eds.), *Personnel selection* and assessment: Individual and organizational perspectives (pp. 235–252). Hillsdale, NJ: Erlbaum.

Ilgen, D. R., & Feldman, J. M. (1983). Performance appraisal: A process focus. In L. Cummings & B. Staw (Eds.), *Research in organizational behavior* (Vol. 5; pp. 349–380). Greenwich CT: JAI.

Ilgen, D. R., Fisher, C. D., & Taylor, M. S. (1979). Consequences of individual feedback on behavior in organizations. *Journal of Applied Psychology, 64*, 347–371.

Johnson, J. (2005). Employees' justice perceptions of performance appraisals systems: Attitudinal, behavioral, and performance consequences. *Journal of Applied Psychology, 79*, 937–939.

Kluger, A. N., & DeNisi, A. S. (1996). The effects of feedback interventions on performance: Historical review, meta-analysis, a preliminary feedback intervention theory. *Psychological Bulletin, 119*, 254–284.

Kluger, A. N., & DeNisi, A. S. (1998). Feedback interventions: Toward the understanding of a double-edge sword. *Current Directions in Psychological Science, 7*, 67–72.

Komaki, J. L. (1998). When performance improvement is the goal: A new set of criteria for criteria. *Journal of Applied Behavior Analysis, 31*, 263–280.

Komaki, J. L., & Minnich, M. R. (2001). Developing performance appraisals: Criteria for what and how performance is measured. In C. M. Johnson, W. K. Redmon, & T. C. Mawhinney (Eds.), *Handbook of organizational performance: Behavior analysis and management* (pp. 51–67). Binghamton, NY: Haworth.

Kozlowski, S. W. J., Gully, S. M., Nason, E. R., & Smith, E. M. (1999). Developing adaptive teams: A theory of compilation and performance over time. In D. R. Ilgen & E. D. Pulakos (Eds.), *The changing nature of work and performance: Implications for staffing, personnel actions, and development* (pp. 240–292). San Francisco, CA: Jossey-Bass.

Landy, F. J., Barnes, J, & Murphy, K. (1978). Correlates of perceived fairness and accuracy in performance appraisal. *Journal of Applied Psychology, 63*, 751–754.

Landy, F. J., & Farr, J. L. (1980). Performance rating. *Psychological Bulletin, 87*, 72–107.

Latane, B., Williams, K., & Harkins, S. (1979). Many hands make light the work: The causes and consequences of social loafing. *Journal of Personality and Social Psychology, 37*, 822–832.

Latham, G. P., Wexley, K. N., & Pursell, E. P. (1975). Training managers to minimize rating errors in the observation of behavior. *Journal of Applied Psychology, 65*, 422–427.

Locke, E. A., & Latham, G. P. (1990). *A theory of goal setting and task performance*. Englewood Cliffs, NJ: Prentice-Hall.

Meyer, H. H., Kay, E., & French, J. R. P. (1965). Split roles in performance appraisals. *Harvard Business Review, 43*, 123–129.

Murphy, K. R., & Balzer, W. K. (1989). Rater errors and rating accuracy. *Journal of Applied Psychology, 74*, 619–624.

Murphy, K. R., & Cleveland, J. N. (1995). *Understanding performance appraisal: Social, organizational, and goal-based perspectives*. Thousand Oaks, CA: Sage.

Naylor, J. C., Pritchard, R. D., & Ilgen, D. R. (1980). *A theory of behavior in organizations*. New York, NY: Academic Press.

Organ, D. (1988). *Organizational citizenship behavior: The good soldier syndrome.* Lexington, MA: Lexington Books.

Porter, C. (2005). Goal orientation: Effects on backing-up behavior, performance, efficacy, and commitment in teams. *Journal of Applied Psychology, 90,* 811–818.

Pritchard, R. D., Holling, H., Lammers, F., & Clark, B. D. (Eds.). (2002). *Improving organizational performance with the Productivity Measurement and Enhancement System: An international collaboration.* Huntington, NY: Nova Science.

Pritchard, R. D., Jones, S. D., Roth, P. L., Steubing, K. K., & Ekeberg, S. E. (1988). The effects of group feedback, goal setting, and incentives on organizational productivity. *Journal of Applied Psychology Monograph, 73,* 337–358.

Pulakos, E. D. (1984). A comparison of rater training programs: Error training and accuracy training. *Journal of Applied Psychology, 69,* 581–588.

Pulakos, E. D. (2004). *A roadmap for developing, implementing, and evaluating performance management systems.* Alexandria, VA: SHRM Foundation.

Pulakos, E. D. (2009). *Performance management: A new approach for driving business results.* Madden, MA: Wiley-Blackwell.

Saavedra, R., Earley, P. C., & Van Dyne, L. (1993). Complex interdependence in task-performing groups. *Journal of Applied Psychology, 78,* 61–71.

Smith, P. C., & Kendall, L. M. (1963). Retranslations of expectations: An approach to the construction of unambiguous anchors for rating scales. *Journal of Applied Psychology, 47,* 149–155.

Smither, J. W. (Ed.). (1998). *Performance appraisal: State of the art in practice.* San Francisco, CA: Jossey-Bass.

Sulsky, L. M., & Balzer, W. K. (1998). The meaning and measurement of performance appraisal accuracy: Some methodological concerns. *Journal of Applied Psychology, 73,* 497–506.

Taylor, M. S., Tracy, K. B., Renard, M. K., Harrison, J. K., & Carroll, S. J. (1995). Due process in performance appraisal: A quasi-experiment in procedural justice. *Administrative Science Quarterly, 40,* 495–523.

Thorndike, E. L. (1920). A constant error in psychological ratings. *Journal of Applied Psychology, 4,* 469–477.

Van Scotter, J. R., Motowidlo, S. J., & Cross, T. C. (2000). Effects of task performance and contextual performance on systematic rewards. *Journal of Applied Psychology, 85,* 526–535.

Varma, A., DeNisi, A. S., & Peters, L. H. (1996). Interpersonal affect in performance appraisal: A field study. *Personnel Psychology, 49,* 341–360.

Weitz, J. (1961). Criteria for criteria. *American Psychologist, 16,* 228–232.

Williams, K. J., DeNisi, A. S., Blencoe, A. G., & Cafferty, T. P. (1985). The role of appraisal purpose: Effects of purpose on information acquisition and utilization. *Organizational Behavior and Human Decision Processes, 35,* 314–339.

Square Pegs and Round Holes: Ruminations on the Relationship Between Performance Appraisal and Performance Management

NICOLE E. GRAVINA and BRIAN P. SIERS

Roosevelt University, Schaumberg, Illinois, USA

Models of comprehensive Performance Management systems include both employee development and evaluative components. The Organizational Behavior Management discipline focuses almost exclusively on the developmental component, while the Industrial and Organizational Psychology discipline is focused on use of performance appraisals. Performance appraisals have several well-documented shortcomings. Despite those limitations, an examination of Performance Management models suggests that they often include an appraisal component. However, there is little consensus on how Performance Management should incorporate appraisals. The authors argue that performance data should be an output of a Performance Management process, not as an input or starting-point for developmental activities. This emphasizes goal-setting, feedback, and coaching throughout the year, and performance data are aggregated to provide enough information about performance to facilitate administrative decision-making when needed. An optimal performance management system that serves both the developmental and administrative functions can be created by carefully combining the approaches of both disciplines.

Hyten (2009) attributed the lack of growth and outside recognition of the field of Organizational Behavior Management (OBM) to the dearth of systemic solutions that focus on impacting business results. He asserted that OBM should learn from the successes achieved with Behavior-Based Safety and, rather than aiming interventions at behaviors that are troubling to frontline managers, the field should develop comprehensive solutions aimed at behaviors that drive business results. Although OBM research has continuously demonstrated success in changing relatively simple work behaviors (e.g., Goomas, 2008; Tittelbach, DeAngelis, Sturmey, & Alvero, 2007), few examples exist of employing a systemic approach that can be applied business-wide to improve organizational functioning and achieve a range of performance management goals simultaneously. In order to be recognized as the leading approach to performance management, OBM must develop and communicate strategies that address a range of performance management issues and can be applied across an entire organization.

The challenge of developing a comprehensive and effective performance management system is not unique to OBM. There is growing interest among researchers and practitioners in Industrial and Organizational (I-O) Psychology to develop more effective performance management systems (Aguinis, 2009). Historically, I-O psychologists have focused on measuring performance quantitatively with performance appraisals. Their struggles measuring and conceptualizing work performance have been collectively termed the *criterion problem* (e.g., Austin & Villanova, 1992). In a recent chapter reviewing the topic, Aguinis (2009) called the collective focus of the I-O field on performance appraisal, "almost an obsession" (p. 1). The field was so consumed with empirical paradigm tinkering that Landy and Farr (1983) famously called for a moratorium on research on performance appraisal response formats. However, the focus of research and practice is changing from the exclusive use of performance appraisal to more comprehensive and developmentally focused performance management processes (e.g., Aguinas, 2009). This trend is so pervasive that Latham and Mann (2006) speculated their review of the performance appraisal literature would be "the last review of the literature where performance appraisal is in the title" (p. 296).

Confusingly, despite both fields settling on the superiority of performance management, this has not meant a move away from the use of performance appraisal in organizations. In fact, performance appraisal is likely a component of many, if not most, performance management processes. Performance appraisals are ubiquitous because they help organizations accomplish two important administrative functions: documenting performance and making comparisons between employees. However, the long-standing attitude that *either* you do performance appraisal *or* you do performance management is disappearing. It seems to be finally accepted that the evaluative component associated with performance appraisal and the developmental aspects of associated with performance management should be intertwined (Latham & Mann, 2006).

In a recent book chapter, Aguinis (2009) asserted that performance management should serve six functions: (a) linking work behaviors to the organization's strategic purposes, (b) serving as a basis for administrative decisions, (c) communicating performance standards and performance feedback to employees, (d) establishing developmental objectives for training and coaching activities, (e) providing data for organization-wide maintenance and interventions, and (f) documenting performance records for organizational and legal purposes. OBM approaches to performance management have focused mainly on the communicative/feedback (c) and developmental functions (d), while I-O approaches have focused on using performance appraisals to generate data for administrative decisions (b) and documenting those decisions (f). We agree with Aguinas that performance management should serve all of these functions. Thus, improving performance management practices will ultimately require some combination of the OBM and I-O approaches.

WHAT IS PERFORMANCE APPRAISAL? WHAT IS PERFORMANCE MANAGEMENT?

Semantic issues in the literature on work performance can make it difficult to determine what the relationship between performance appraisal and performance management is (or should be). For example, one of the difficulties associated with reviewing the I-O literature on work performance is that writers often use performance management as a synonym for traditional performance appraisal. It is not uncommon to learn of "bare bones" performance management processes that really just consist of a traditional annual performance appraisal (Silverman & Muller, 2009, p. 527). Thus, before discussing how the two approaches might be integrated, we thought it best to start with a brief discussion and description of performance appraisal and performance management. For a further description and discussion of performance management processes, see DeNisi (2011) in this volume.

As the title of a landmark book about performance appraisal would suggest (Landy & Farr, 1983), performance appraisal is focused on the measurement of work performance. Its mission is to take a "snapshot" of work performance. Performance appraisals typically involve a combination of subjective ratings of performance and use of "objective" performance indices (Landy & Farr, 1983). To the dismay of OBM researchers and practitioners who understand the value of frequent feedback (e.g., Komaki, 1998), this appraisal process is traditionally conducted too infrequently (annual, biannual, quarterly, etc.) and is too vague to improve and sustain performance (Daniels, 2009).

I-O psychologists recognize and have extensively researched the limitations of performance appraisal, particularly subjective measures of performance. There are several psychometric problems with subjective appraisals of performance like halo error (Viswesvaran, Schmidt, & Ones, 2005) and poor reliability (Viswesvaran, Ones, & Schmidt, 1996). Ratee perceptions of the process are often poor as well. Employees often ". . . [believe] that they are being evaluated on the wrong things, by the wrong person; that is, the person who is evaluating them lacks objectivity, and hence is not 'fair'" (Latham, Almost, Mann, & Moore, 2005, p. 77). This perceived lack of procedural fairness can have ranging negative implications for organizations (Cohen-Charash & Spector, 2001; Colquitt, Conlon, Wesson, Porter, & Ng, 2001).

Recognizing the problems associated with the use of supervisor ratings of subordinate work performance, a trend toward using "objective" criteria was observed in the 1960's (Austin & Villanova, 1992). Commonly used objective criteria include countable or verifiable events like production/sales data, turnover, absenteeism, disciplinary write-ups, or accidents. Interestingly, objective criteria are robustly correlated with subjective supervisor ratings of performance ($\rho = .39$), though the relationship is not strong enough for the measures to be viewed as interchangeable (Bommer, Johnson, Rich, Podsakoff, & Mackenzie, 1995). Although appealing because these criteria involve less subjectivity than supervisor ratings of performance dimensions, they are not without their well-documented drawbacks (Landy & Farr, 1983). Each of these "objective" criteria can be differentially deficient or contaminated depending on the situation and job in question. This greatly complicates their systematized use. For example, it is difficult to compare individuals on dollar or unit levels of sales performance because there are many variables outside of the employee's control that influence this criterion (Latham, et al., 2005).

Given the drawbacks with subjective and objective approaches to operationalizing job performance, one might think that direct observations of performance are the solution. However, direct observations of behavior are conceptually problematic as well. Even direct observations of performance often require observers to make judgments based on operational definitions, which may introduce subjectivity. In addition, even well-defined observation criteria can miss the true essence of a behavior. For example, in measuring customer service, the difference between a friendly or an off-putting greeting or smile is difficult to operationalize. In other words, subjective ratings play an important role when measuring performance that is difficult to precisely and practically define and still retain the intention behind including it. Even so, direct observation can provide very useful information if it can be practically implemented in the workplace. However, given the amount of time and access required to conduct direct observations, it is clear that results-based objective measures, self-recording, and ratings may also be necessary to capture a complete picture of performance and aid in the larger task of performance management.

Performance management is defined as a "continuous process of identifying, measuring, and developing the performance of individuals and teams and aligning performance with the strategic goals of the organization" (Aguinas, 2009, p. 2). Regular feedback about performance is essential, directly addressing the aforementioned complaint about the infrequency of performance appraisal. In addition to providing performance feedback, developmental "coaching is inherent in the process" (Latham & Mann, 2006, p. 296). Thus, performance management widens the performance measurement focus of traditional performance appraisal to include a greater emphasis on employee development.

OBSTACLES TO INTEGRATING PERFORMANCE APPRAISAL AND PERFORMANCE MANAGEMENT

Although performance appraisals alone may not inspire peak performance and discretionary effort, they do help accomplish two important organizational goals of performance management— making administrative decisions and documenting performance. I-O psychologists have designed performance appraisals to make distinctions among employees based on their performance. In organizations and in life, opportunities and resources are scarce. Guion (1998) echoes the view of most I-O psychologists that merit-based decision making is considered the fair method of allocating scarce opportunity and resources; this requires "methods for establishing relative merit" (p. 7). To facilitate this, I-O psychologists tend to view job performance as an individual difference variable (Bucklin, Alvero, Dickinson, Austin, & Jackson, 2000). All organizations inevitably have to make these administrative decisions. Title VII of the Civil Rights Act of 1964 made it illegal to discriminate based on protected characteristics (sex, race, religion, color, national origin; age, family status, and genetic content were added later) when recruiting, training, promoting/demoting, terminating, or making compensation decisions. Thus, performance "snap shots" allow these decisions to be made legally using job-related data. However, the administrative focus of performance appraisals can breed employee resentment and frustration with the appraisal process, thus shifting the focus away from employee development.

Administrative goals need to be balanced with developmental goals if a performance management system is going to provide maximum value to an organization and its employees. The OBM approach can help achieve this balance through its focus on encouraging "personal bests rather than best persons" (Crowell, 2005, p. 201). This emphasis on within-person change is likely essential for employee development. Standards of performance required to ensure organizational success should be identified, and all employees should be given equal opportunity and support to meet or exceed those standards, regardless of the performance of others. In other words, a good performance management system should not limit employee development in order to accomplish other goals.

OBM and I-O research has identified other important factors for developing and improving employee performance, namely regular feedback and consequences. A review by Alvero, Bucklin, and Austin (2001) identified numerous research studies that demonstrated consistent improvements in performance after feedback was implemented. Recognizing success (e.g., Ellis & Dividi, 2005), monetary incentives (e.g., LaMere, Dickinson, Henry, Henry, & Poling, 1996), and coaching (e.g., Yu, Collins, Cavanagh, White, & Fairbrother, 2008) have also been demonstrated to be important components of performance improvement interventions and therefore should become a fixture of every performance management process. In sum, the best performance management process incorporates components that embody the positive elements of both approaches. Blending I-O's emphasis on fairness and minimizing legal exposures with OBM's emphasis on the development of each employee (rather than sorting employees into categories) results in an approach that is likely to appease and motivate the multiple stakeholders in the performance management process.

A key consideration in the design of performance management process must be how to identify the elements of performance that should be measured, evaluated, and developed. I-O psychologists encourage the use of a systematic process of job analysis to define the performance domain (Austin, Villanova, & Hindman, 1995). It is also a legal requirement that many human resource management functions (like performance appraisal) be based on job data. For example, the *Uniform Guidelines* mandate that a job analysis underlie performance evaluations, though some objective criteria like production rates and absenteeism can be used without a job analysis "if the user can show the importance of the criteria to the particular employment context" (*Uniform Guidelines*, Section 14B[3]) presumably through validity information.

OBM researchers and practitioners argue that effective performance improvement solutions focus on a few of the most important objectively measureable behaviors and results that contribute to the strategic goals of the job, department, and organization (Daniels & Daniels, 2004; Gilbert, 1978). By focusing on the most strategically-related aspects of performance, the OBM approach may not capture valuable aspects of employee performance (e.g., due to criterion deficiency). For example, two employees may perform similarly on an objective measure of productivity. However, one employee may exhibit discretionary effort by improving the work process or supporting and training new employees. Failure to formally document these aspects of performance may result in a deserving employee missing out on opportunities for recognition, promotion, or merit-based pay increases. In addition, a measurement system that does not widely document performance may result in an inadequate evaluation of the effectiveness of performance improvement solutions.

However, these approaches are far from mutually exclusive. Many organizations now use competency modeling instead of job analysis as a basis for the creation of performance appraisals. These competency models focus on the competencies that are required across the organization and related to organization-level objectives (Shippmann et al., 2000). Though the legality of competency modeling has not yet been well-defined by the courts as a substitute for a thorough job analysis, it nevertheless provides a tool for performance managers to use when determining what performance dimensions are most important in a given work role. Further, a simple process of "mapping" job tasks onto a competency model would highlight job tasks most related to those organization-level objectives. The performance management process could focus on those tasks determined to be most important. Then, performance data could comprise information collected through developing a few of the most important behaviors. Of course, this is easier said than done. Many case studies document the difficulties associated with trying to identify behavioral indices of certain key job tasks (e.g., Komaki, 1998). However, OBM models like Komaki and Reynard Minnich's (2001) "SURF and C" model have provided guidelines for selecting work behaviors for evaluation purposes.

HOW SHOULD PERFORMANCE APPRAISAL AND PERFORMANCE MANAGEMENT BE INTEGRATED?

Ultimately, performance appraisal has and will continue to play an important role in performance management processes. However, given the limitations of the way performance appraisals are typically implemented, they should not be considered the baseline for a comprehensive performance management system to build upon. In other words, a performance appraisal should not be an *input* to a performance management system, but rather an *output* or summary of behavioral and performance data collected as part of a performance management process.

This distinction has important implications. If performance appraisal is an *input*, a perspective commonly held by I-O psychologists, then the appraisal serves as the primary source or summary of performance data for the performance management process. Appraisal is an event where data are collected, organized, and presented on forms. Then other performance management activities (goal setting, coaching, etc.) occur separately to improve performance. Here the performance appraisal acts as a benchmark used to assess change in performance *and* compare the performance of the employee to other employees.

However, if performance appraisal is an *output* of the performance management process, then the process occurs differently. The process cycle does not begin or end with assessment, but with communication of performance dimensions, goal-setting for those dimensions, and a discussion of the behaviors that relate to those performance dimensions. Then, performance data are gathered continually throughout the year. Objective data, direct observation data, critical incidents, and subjective rating data can be routinely added to a database. Regular meetings can be scheduled to review the current performance data and update performance standards and goals as needed, as well as to provide coaching and feedback. Here, the appraisal "instrument" is essentially a summary of the data that are being continually collected, facilitating developmental efforts throughout the year. Examples of this approach can include the use of balanced scorecards and performance dashboards. Viewing performance appraisal as an output still facilitates making administrative decisions and still allows for legal compliance, but from the perspective of the subordinate, the emphasis has shifted from assessment to development.

One can see how technology could greatly aid this becoming a reality in organizations. The dreaded performance appraisal form might become a thing of the past. Instead, it is easy to imagine performance data being input into websites and "performance dashboards" dynamically generating performance indices that can be used for between-person comparisons, administrative decision making, and enhancing employee development efforts. Further, this approach would facilitate another important use of performance appraisal—for use in the validation of selection procedures (Landy & Farr, 1983).

By combining the strengths of OBM and I/O into one comprehensive performance management system, the bad baggage associated with each approach can be minimized. For example, concerns about the practicality of direct behavior observations and rater errors can be minimized by borrowing from the world of performance appraisal and including behaviorally focused rating scales (Latham, Fay, & Saari, 1979) or even some subjective performance data. Administrative and legal functions of the process are upheld, and reactions to the process will likely improve because performance management works. An effective process will go a long way to improve the poor reactions often associated with performance management and focus managers on an important but often forgotten part of their job—management. A formalized system should require and reward supervisor's provision of feedback and coaching to employees on a regular basis. In fact, feedback and coaching should be an important part of the performance evaluation process for every supervisor.

It is intimidating to attempt to add a substantive point to the mountains of research and accumulated practical wisdom about performance appraisal and performance management. We humbly submit that performance appraisal is best conceptualized and implemented as an output and not an input of the performance management process. This approach meets the traditionally distinct performance management foci of both the I-O and OBM camps. Moving forward, we hope that special issues like this one, I-O involvement in OBM conferences (and vice-versa), and broadening the training perspective in graduate programs places a focus on leveraging the strengths of all approaches to create effective solutions. After all, our clients deserve the state of the art, not dogma related to our discipline.

REFERENCES

Aguinis, H. (2009). An expanded view of performance management. In J. W. Smither & M. London (Eds.), *Performance management: Putting research into action* (pp. 1–44). San Francisco, CA: Jossey-Bass.

Alvero, A., Bucklin, B., & Austin, J. (2001). An objective review of the effectiveness and essential characteristics of performance feedback in organizational settings (1985–1998). *Journal of Organizational Behavior Management, 21*(1), 3–30.

Austin, J. T., & Villanova, P. (1992). The criterion problem: 1917–1992. *Journal of Applied Psychology, 77*, 836–874.

Austin, J. T., Villanova, P., & Hindman, H. D. (1995). Legal requirements and technical guidelines involved in implementing performance appraisal systems. In G. R. Ferris & M. R. Buckley (Eds.), *Human resource management: Perspectives, context, functions, and outcomes* (3rd ed.; pp. 63–77). Boston, MA: Allyn & Bacon.

Bommer, W. H., Johnson, J. L., Rich, G. A., Podsakoff, P. M., & Mackenzie, S. B. (1995). On the interchangeability of objective and subjective measures of employee performance: A meta-analysis. *Personnel Psychology, 48*, 587–605.

Bucklin, B. R., Alvero, A. M., Dickinson, A. M., Austin, J., & Jackson, A. K. (2000). Industrial-Organizational Psychology and Organizational Behavior Management: An objective comparison. *Journal of Organizational Behavior Management, 20*(2), 27–75.

Cohen-Charash, Y., & Spector, P. E. (2001). The role of justice in organizations: A meta-analysis. *Organizational Behavior and Human Decision Processes, 86*(2), 278–321.

Colquitt, J. A., Conlon, D. E., Wesson, M. J., Porter, C., & Ng, K.Y. (2001). Justice at the Millennium: A meta-analytic review of 25 years of organizational justice research. *Journal of Applied Psychology, 86*(3), 425–445.

Crowell, C. R. (2005). Beyond positive reinforcement: OBM as a humanizing approach to management practices. *Journal of Organizational Behavior Management, 24*(1/2), 195–202.

Daniels, A. C. (2009). *Oops! 13 management practices that waste time and money (and what to do instead)*. Atlanta, GA: Performance Management Publications.

Daniels, A. C., & Daniels, J. E. (2004). *Performance management: Changing behavior that drives organizational effectiveness* (4th ed). Atlanta, GA: Performance Management Publications.

DeNisi, A. (2011). Managing performance to change behavior. *Journal of Organizational Behavior Management, 31*(4), 262–276.

Ellis, S., & Davidi, I. (2005). After-event reviews: Drawing lessons from successful and failed experience. *Journal of Applied Psychology, 90*, 857–871.

Gilbert, T. F. (1978). *Human competence: Engineering worthy performance*. New York, NY: McGraw-Hill.

Goomas, D. T. (2008). The effects of computerized auditory feedback on electronic article surveillance tag placement in an auto-distribution center. *Journal of Organizational Behavior Management, 28*, 188–197.

Guion, R. (1998). *Assessment, measurement, and prediction for personnel decisions*. Mahwah, NJ: Erlbaum.

Hyten, C. (2009). Strengthening the focus of business results: The need for systems approaches in organizational behavior management. *Journal of Organizational Behavior Management, 29*, 87–107.

Komaki, J. L. (1998). When performance improvement is the goal: A new set of criteria for criteria. *Journal of Applied Behavior Analysis, 31*(2), 263–280.

Komaki, J. L., & Reynard Minnich, M. (2001). Developing performance appraisals: Criteria for what and how performance is measured. In C. M. Johnson, W. K. Redmon, & T. C. Mawhinney (Eds.), *Handbook of organizational performance: Behavior analysis and management* (pp. 51–80). New York, NY: Haworth.

Landy, F. J., & Farr, J. L. (1983). *The measurement of work performance*. New York, NY: Academic Press.

Latham, G. P., Almost, J., Mann, S., & Moore, C. (2005). New developments in performance management. *Organizational Dynamics, 34*(1), 77–87.

Latham, G. P., Fay, C. H., & Saari, L. M. (1979). The development of behavioral observation scales for appraising the performance of foremen. *Personnel Psychology, 32*, 299–311.

Latham, G. P., & Mann S. (2006). Advances in the science of performance appraisal: Implications for practice. *International Review of Industrial and Organizational Psychology, 21*, 295–337.

LaMere, J. M., Dickinson, A. M., Henry, M., Henry, G., & Poling, A. (1996) Effects of a multi-component monetary incentive program on the performance of truck drivers: A longitudinal study. *Behavior Modification, 20*, 385–406.

Murphy, K. R., & Cleveland, J. N. (1991). *Performance appraisal: An organizational perspective*. Needham Heights, MA: Allyn & Bacon.

Shippmann, J. S., Ash, R. A., Batjtsta, M.., Carr, L., Eyde, L. D., Hesketh, B., . . . Sanchez, J. I. (2000). The practice of competency modeling. *Personnel Psychology, 53*, 703–740.

Silverman, S. B., & Muller, W. M. (2009). Assessing performance management programs and policies. In J. W. Smither & M. London, (Eds.), *Performance management: Putting research into action* (pp. 527–554). San Francisco, CA: Jossey-Bass.

Tittelbach, D., DeAngelis, M., Sturmey, P., & Alvero, A. M. (2007). The effects of task clarification, feedback, and goal setting on student advisors' office behaviors and customer service. *Journal of Organizational Behavior Management, 27*(3), 27–40.

Uniform guidelines on employee selection procedures. (1978). 43 Fed. Reg. 38, 290-38, 315.

Viswesvaran, C., Ones, D. S., & Schmidt, F. L. (1996). Comparative analysis of the reliability of job performance ratings. *Journal of Applied Psychology, 81*, 557–574.

Viswesvaran, C., Schmidt, F. L., & Ones, D. S. (2005). Is there a general factor in ratings of job performance? A meta-analytic framework for disentangling substantive and error influences. *Journal of Applied Psychology, 90*(1), 108–131.

Yu, N., Collins, C. G., Cavanagh, M., White, K., & Fairbrother, G. (2008). Positive coaching with frontline managers: Enhancing their effectiveness and understanding why. *International Coaching Psychology Review, 3*(2), 110–122.

Job Satisfaction: I/O Psychology and Organizational Behavior Management Perspectives

THOMAS C. MAWHINNEY
University of Detroit Mercy, Detroit, Michigan, USA

Perspectives on job satisfaction and its relations with job performance among members of the Industrial/Organizational Psychology (IOP) and Organizational Behavior Management (OBM) cultures are identified and compared. Comparisons include vantage points of each culture on the roles of theory and data regarding the definitions of behavior, job performance, job satisfaction, and the potential causal relations among them. Literature reviewed suggests the IOP culture has validated technologies that some members of the OBM culture recognize as useful for purposes of assessing what members of the OBM culture call Social Validity (SV). Given similarities among values of the two cultures, reflected in their mutual concern for assessing Organizational Responsibility and SV, the author proffers the following recommendation: Members of the OBM culture should not eschew the IOP culture's practices that might contribute to OBM practitioners' ability to effectively establish the SV of their interventions, particularly large-scale interventions.

WHAT I/O PSYCHOLOGY AND OBM DO AND DO NOT HAVE IN COMMON

Members of the Industrial and Organizational Psychology (IOP) and Organizational Management Behavior (OBM) *cultures* (Glenn, 1991; Mawhinney, 1992, 2001; Redmon & Agnew, 1991, Redmon & Mason, 2001; Redmon & Wilk, 1991) have professed similar *values* (cf. Diefendorff & Chandler, 2010; Skinner, 1974). They include contributing to the health and welfare among people with whom the cultures may be involved (cf. Aguinis, 2010; Dickinson, 2000; Dubin, 1976, pp. 22–23; Dunnette, 1976, p. viii; Mawhinney, 1984, 1989; Miller, 1980, p. 145).

Thus, IOP and OBM share, in a very general way, perspectives regarding "antecedents" and "outcomes" of job satisfaction (JS) among formal organization (FO) members. How they conceptualize, assess, and manage JS-job performance (JP) relationships, on the other hand, varies between the two cultures. This article explores important historical and contemporary perspectives of the IOP and OBM cultures as they relate to the concepts of JS and, unavoidably, its role in various conceptions and dimensions of JP among members of FOs. These perspectives are implicitly or explicitly juxtaposed in terms of Wertheimer's (1972) *Fundamental Issues in Psychology*. Variations on Wertheimer's themes provide a succinct comparison of IOP's and OBM's perspectives on JS, and the tacit issue concerning JS's role in human behavior and performance.

A BRIEF INTRODUCTION TO GRAND THEORIES OF IOP AND OBM

On Wertheimer's dimension of *theory versus data,* IOP is strongly oriented toward theory while OBM is more, and in some instances, virtually solely data oriented *at this time*. Yet, IOP and OBM each possesses what might be called a grand theory or overarching general theory of organizational members' behavior and its relationship with performance. The theories differ from one another in important ways. Two important facets are classes of behavior and psychological constructs; JS and JP reflect these differences.

What Is Behavior From the IOP Perspective?

According to Zedeck (2010), "*Behavior* is often defined as 'observable actions,' *but I/O psychologists study more than observable actions*" [emphasis added] (p. xxii). They study a host of person-centric constructs too, such as values, attitudes, and abilities believed to be related to what persons think and do in work settings (Zedeck, 2010). These variables/constructs are often used to understand why people do what they do in terms of their grand theory and theories in more limited domains, for example, theories of work motivation, performance, and satisfaction, such as Vroom's (1964) classic cognitive theory of work motivation.

What Is IOP's Grand Theory?

The IOP culture has implicitly adopted a grand theory rooted in the work of Kurt Lewin (1935). Lewin's expression: $B = f(P,E)$, where B = observable behavior (or frequently a construct, B_c), P = the person's inferred psychological activities (constructs, P_c, e.g., needs, self-efficacy, and job satisfaction) that may include E = the current and/or future "cognized" state(s) of the person's environment so $E = E_c$ = a cognitive construct (cf. Vroom, 1964). All of these variables change as the person responds to and/or acts upon his/her E, at any given moment, *but explicitly not in the past or history. Any effects of history reside in the condition of P or P_c at some moment in time relative to the person's cognized E*. This suggests a grand theory stated as follows in terms of IOP constructs used to measure $B = f(P,E)$: $B_c = f(P_c, E_c)$. Lewin was committed to the idea that behavior is a function (f) of psychological variables related to the person, P, contemporaneous with those various states of E.

Vroom's Expectancy Theory as an Exemplar of an IOP Theory of Motivation and Satisfaction

Vroom (1964) characterized the "central problem of motivation as the explanation of choices made by organisms among different voluntary responses" (p. 9). Vroom spurned Hull's theory (1943, 1951) and drew primarily upon the works of Tolman (1932) and Lewin (1935, 1938) who, according to Vroom, considered Hull's stimulus-response-reinforcement theories insufficient "to account for the more complex aspects of choice behavior" (p. 13). Vroom drew heavily upon Tolman and Lewin for his fundamental presuppositions about the nature of his subjects, terms, and concepts in his theory. Individuals were assumed to be capable of cognitions as internal representations of their environments, evidenced in learning as changing beliefs learned without benefit of "reinforcement." His theory would be ahistoric in Lewin's tradition of Galilean as opposed to an historic Aristotelian mode of "thinking." Vroom recognized that Lewin appreciated the complementary nature of historical and ahistorical accounts of behavior and therefore, de facto, his thinking in this regard reflects Skinner's (1966a) insights into the role of the history of consequences that change the responding organism at a moment in time as a changed organism. But Vroom opted for an ahistoric or Galilean account, and his book is devoid of any reference to Skinner's works. In principle, at least, this strategy obviates the need to take account of a complex individual history when explaining a choice at a moment in time. That is, the ahistoric approach permits one to assess and explain the individual's choices at a given moment in terms of the person's "motives and cognitions at the time he makes the choice" (p. 14).

Vroom's (1964) theory is often referred to as a V-I-E or valence, instrumentality, expectancy theory of work motivation. These psychological terms are hypothesized to be combined in ways that result in forces of attraction or repulsion relative to perceived future consequence or outcome of choices made at some moment in time. For pragmatic reasons, Vroom distinguished between two components of the theory using two propositions, one concerning "sets of actions," and the other "sets of outcomes" of those actions. In Vroom's words,

> We use the term action to refer to *behavior* [emphasis added] which might reasonably be expected to be within the repertoire of the person, e.g., seeking entry into an occupation, while the term outcomes will be reserved for more temporally distant events which are less likely to be under complete behavioral control, e.g., attaining membership in an occupation. (1964, p. 19)

The force acting on a person to choose some *act i*, like choosing a level of effort to exert performing one's job, depends on the sum of *valent outcomes j* (V_j) associated with that choice or *act i* times the expectation that that *act i* will be followed by outcome j, that is: $F_i = f_i [\Sigma\ E_{ij}\ V_j]$ $F_i =$ force to perform *act i* (choose a level of effort); $E_{ij} =$ strength of the expectancy ($0 \leq E_{ij} \leq 1.0$) and $V_j =$ valence of outcome j (adapted from Vroom, 1964, p. 17). If either V_j or $E_{ij} = 0$, then there will be no force to exert effort on the task. A simple example of E_{ij} would occur when my task assignment was to lift, unaided by anyone else or any technology, a 1,000-pound object over my head. But, how could $V_j =$ zero? It could since Vroom defined V_j as $V_j = f_j [\Sigma\ I_{jk}\ V_k]$ (adapted from Vroom, 1964), "where $I_{jk} =$ the cognized instrumentality ($-1 \leq I_{jk} \leq 1$) of outcome j for the attainment of outcome k" (p. 17). Now imagine that there are five valent outcomes with negative instrumentalities and five with positive instrumentalities that have equal valences. Even though all the outcomes are positively valent, V_k, half those with negative instrumentalities reduce the attraction of the V_j by the same amount as those contributing positively to it. The $V_j = f_j [\Sigma\ I_{jk}\ V_k]$ equation might reasonably be called a representation of anticipated satisfaction of *act i*. In a work setting a person might be called upon to decide which action to take and when to take it during a work day, and although produced in part by its role in

V_j, the action might or might not map directly into verbal reports of job satisfaction, as will be noted later.

It may be tempting to conclude that reported levels of JS should be positively correlated with the Valence (V_j) component of V-I-E theory and JP. While V_j and verbal reports of JS should be correlated (Mawhinney, 1989), correlations between JS and JP can range from near zero to relatively high depending on other conditions of the work environment (Table 4.1 of Schleicher, Hansen, & Fox, 2010).

What Is Job Satisfaction (Beyond V-I-E Theory) From the IOP Perspective?

P. C. Smith (1967) defined JS "as an affective response of the worker to his job... [and is] ... similar in meaning to *pleasure*" (p. 343; emphasis added). She went on to lament "the fact that there is no *necessary* connection between productivity and satisfaction" (p. 343). Schleicher, Hansen, and Fox (2010) recognize another two definitions of satisfaction involving affect and emotion: first, Locke's (1969) conception of it as a "state resulting from an employee's perception that his or her job allowed for the fulfillment of his or her values," and Cranny, Smith, and Stone (1992) characterized JS as "an emotional state resulting from an employee's comparison of actual and desired job outcomes" (p. 148). The second approach identified by Schleicher et al. (2010; citing Rosenberg & Hoveland, 1960) characterizes JS "as an attitude, rather than (and distinct from) an emotional state."

Job attitudes are not behavior, rather they are "*personal construct*[s] [P_cs] [emphasis added] that can be used to *describe people* [emphasis added]" (Zedeck, 2010, p. xxii). And these constructs, manifest as scores on JS surveys, play the role of P_c in IOP's grand theory. Often, performance behavior, B_c, is measured by supervisors' ratings (Schleicher et al., 2010, p. 153, Table 4.1). Note behavior may itself be a construct. *Organizational citizenship behavior* (OCB) is a construct, B_c, typically assessed via paper and pencil responses about behavior descriptions on rating scales (Organ, Podsakoff, & MacKenzie, 2006), rather than tangible behavior per se or tangible consequences of behavior in the traditions of OBM (Gilbert, 1978). Attitudes are also measured via another class of behavior, verbal behavior (Baum, 2005; Hayes, Bond, & Barns-Holmes, 2006; Malott, 1992; Skinner, 1957), again usually in the form of paper and pencil or computer screens, keyboards, mice, and/or microphones and earphones.

Some JS scales measure satisfaction with facets of the job, and some measure global satisfaction with the job. There exist well-developed and accepted procedures in IOP for establishing their validity and reliability (Locke, Smith, Kendall, Hulin, & Miller, 1964; Smith, 1967; Stone-Romero,

2010). Twenty-six (26) JS scales were summarized by Robinson, Athanasiou, and Head (1969). The two most popular among current measures are the *Job Descriptive Index (JDI)* and the *Minnesota Satisfaction Questionnaire (MSQ)* (Schleicher et al., 2010).

As described in detail above, Vroom's (1964) valence-instrumentality-expectancy theory of motivational force (MF) was created to explain how and why employees choose a level of effort to expend on achievement of some level of performance. As such, it is a theory regarding predicted effects of *anticipated future satisfaction from choices among current levels of effort to expend in the pursuit of performance*. Vroom has argued that in some cases verbal reports may not be the only, but are often the most, practical means of assessing valence. That being the case, a self-reported measure of job related valence, and de facto JS, "*is the conceptual equivalent of the valence of the job or work role to the person performing it* [emphasis added]" (p. 101).

Variations of Vroom's V-I-E theory have been elaborated and used in many work research domains, including leadership (e.g., House's version of path goal leadership, 1971) and creation of jobs designed to simultaneously increase job performance and satisfaction (cf. Hackman and Oldham's job characteristics model of intrinsic motivation, 1980). The House leadership model includes two intrinsic motivation components: one for task behavior per se and one for task accomplishments. However, to the extent that this class of theory depends critically on verbal reports, these Vroom-type variables resolve to the following behavioral relationships with JS and JP within the IOP culture: $B_{observed\ behavior} = f(MF_c)$, where MF_c = the products of several V-I-E constructs (Mitchell, 1974; Pinder, 2008). Notice that E_c (as in $B_c = f(P_c, E_c)$) is not explicitly in this expression. This is because no matter what the objective environment, the cognized states of the current and future environment, according to V-I-E theories, are determinants of each level of motivational forces to choose some level of work effort. These MFs *are subjective outcomes of subjective assessment processes* hypothesized to take place *within* the individual decision maker.

To summarize, the IOP culture tends toward being theory-oriented such that theories dictate and drive decisions about data and its uses, is highly concerned with "understanding" behavior from the *subjective vantage point of people whose thoughts and feelings are to be understood in relation to work performance*, and is focused primarily on *perceptions* of present and future relationships between thoughts and behavior. IOP's theoretical/psychological constructs and measures provide the *practical implications* of understanding the world of work through the lenses of their theories and assumptions regarding the "nature" of homo sapiens (Eberly, Holtom, Lee, & Mitchell, 2009; Judge & Klinger, 2009; Locke, 2009; Rosseau, 2009).

WHY MEASURE JOB SATISFACTION FROM EITHER CULTURE'S PERSPECTIVE?

Whether and how JS leads to job performance remains a controversial question among some academics (cf. Cherrington, Reitz, & Scott, 1971; Judge, Thoresen, Bono, & Patton, 2001, p. 379). Results and conclusions drawn from a meta-analysis by Riketta (2008) notwithstanding, Smith (1967) contended: "It is not really meaningful to ask why pleasure or satisfaction are good or desirable. They are desirable by nature" (p. 344). Hantula and Kondash (2007) support the following proposition regarding rights and responsibilities: "Demonstrated control of work environment[s] implies responsibility for [them] . . . . *Improving* affective reaction to work is within . . . [the] . . . realm [of our control] and [therefore] becomes our duty" (p. 15). Smith discussed a perennial duo of organizational problems, absenteeism and turnover, noting perhaps these two as the most obvious objective and valid outcomes associated with JS in spite of their low correlations with satisfaction across a host of scales and meta-analytic relationships, in this case outcomes of job satisfaction (Schleicher et al., 2010, pp. 150–154). Table 4.1 of Schleicher et al. (2010) reports the following "observed sample-weighted average correlation[s] (mean r) between . . ." job-satisfaction and two outcomes: (a) absenteeism for two r's of respectively −.12 ($k=2$ samples) and −.17 ($k=25$ samples); and (b) turnover for five r's of respectively −.14 ($k=7$ samples), −.17 ($k=67$ samples), −.19 ($k=67$ samples), −.16 ($k=19$ samples), and −.14 ($k=49$ samples; where $k=$ meta-analytic samples). These low correlations are surely at least in part a function of large numbers of employees in diverse work settings whose work lives are filled with Hobson's Choices. (Hobson rented horses in 1700s England. "He did so on the condition that one took the horse he assigned *or no horse at all* [emphasis added]" [Starr, 1971, p. 616, fn 46].)

WHY ARE SATISFACTION-RELATED-CRITERIA CORRELATIONS SO LOW? PERSPECTIVES, THEORIES, AND SOME IOP AND OBM DATA

Hobson's Choice (i.e., only one option or alternative) accounts for some to all of the insensitivity of performance ratings to changes in magnitude of valent antecedents and/or outcomes (potential reinforcers); but see Landy (1978) and, in particular see Bowling, Beehr, Wagner, and Libkuman (2005) who suggest a diametrically opposite theory: "In short, job satisfaction may be stable because enduring individual differences predispose people to consistently choose and be selected into particular kinds of work environments" (p. 1045). The implication of the Hobson's Choice argument is that both stability and low values of JS correlations across time are due to the absence of participants' choices among jobs, while Bowling et al. (2005) suggest that these results arise from histories of participants or organizational members' choices among jobs and point to data in support of this position. The OBM theory also applies to values of cumulative (or molar) outcomes of work even when the outcomes are contingent on performance rates (Catania, 1963; Mawhinney, 1982), assessed over appreciable periods of time during which understanding is evident in the researchers' ability to control the phenomenon under investigation (Baer, Wolf, & Risley, 1968; Daniels, 1977; Komaki & Goltz, 2001; Sidman, 1960). The IOP theory pivots on the presence of readily available job choices, while the OBM theory pivots on their absence among organizational members.

Further, Hobson's Choices, or *absence of discretion* regarding job-related behavior and performance rates chosen by FOs' members, result in *potentially severe restriction of range effects in assessments* of JS and its *outcomes* (Schleicher et al., 2010, pp. 153–154).

F. J. Smith (1977) reported JS and attendance rates differed among managers of the same company on the same day in two different cities. A severe snow storm in Chicago, however, temporarily removed constraints typical in normal situations. The storm provided a valid excuse or "cover" for absences on that day. Hobson's Choice conditions, no good external excuse for absences (i.e., no storm), prevailed on the same day in New York City. This resulted in strong correlations of satisfaction across six job facets with absence among employees in Chicago compared to low and nonsignificant correlations among employees in New York on that day (Smith, 1977). The highest job facet correlation in the *absence* of Hobson's Choice or presences of "real choice" conditions in Chicago was .60 for "job future." Average correlation-point difference between Chicago and New York, among the six facets measured, was *.35 percentage points.* Even if JS per se does not cause performance (in this case, absenteeism), it is surely in a reciprocal relationship with it (Cherrington et al., 1971; Lawler & Porter, 1967; Porter & Lawler, 1968). From a pragmatic vantage point, JS *may* well serve as an organizational performance barometer (Cascio & Boudreau, 2008) and should be of interest to both the IOP and OBM cultures (Mawhinney, 1984, 1989).

Besides JS, another common construct used as a criterion in IOP is psychological strain (psychological ill health states of employees; Beehr, Jex, & Ghosh, 2001). And with respect to job satisfaction and strain as elements of social validity (SV; discussed in more detail later in their study), the −.44 correlation between job satisfaction and job strain reported by Beehr, Glaser, Canali, and Wallwey (2001) supports the argument that lower job satisfaction is associated with higher psychological strain. Further support for this conclusion appears as a −.39 mean r for "Strains (Generic Psychological)" as an "Outcome" of job satisfaction reported in Table 4.1 (p. 154) by Schleicher et al. (2010). As I suggested nearly 30 years ago (Mawhinney, 1984), *OBM researchers and practitioners should collect job satisfaction data and consider taking actions to improve it whenever reasonable and feasible*, if not because it is a humane thing to do, then *because its effects find their way to the organizational bottom line* (Cascio & Boudreau, 2008).

PRACTICAL IMPLICATIONS OF IOP'S ASSESSMENTS OF JOB SATISFACTION AND CRITERION VARIABLE RESULTS

Schleicher et al. (2010) remarked, "Job attitudes and work values are antecedents to [*causes of?*] important individual organizational outcomes, such as performance and retention of employees . . . job attitudes are frequently considered to be important outcomes in and of themselves in the *science* [emphasis added] and practice of I/O psychology" (p. 137).

Members of the IOP culture explain behavior of individuals in FOs based on large numbers of participants, with virtually no attention paid to specific individuals' behavior. This does not reflect Lewin's (1935) Galilean vantage point and aversion to grouped or average data as opposed to analyses of P by E interactions on a person-by-person basis, much as in the origins of behavior analysis (Skinner, 1956). Apparently, generalizable results are preferred to Lewin's preference for understanding individual cases of P by E interactions on a case-by-case basis. Members of the OBM culture recognize this as 180 degrees opposite in terms of norms, values, and practices espoused by behavior analysis. However, OBM currently seeks to promote large-scale interventions and therefore, de facto, emulate a few IOP practices (cf. Hopkins, 1995, 1996).

Schleicher et al. (2010) reported large numbers of samples, ranging from 2 to 879, and large numbers of participants, ranging from 316 to 490,624, for meta-analytic results in their Table 4.1. These sizes insured statistical significance of their correlations, unless truly zero. These correlations can be very useful in that they are provided for antecedents [*causes?*], correlates, and outcomes of JS. The highest among the 154 reported was $r = .64$ JS as a correlate of *organizational commitment*.

WHAT IS BEHAVIOR FROM THE OBM PERSPECTIVE?

"Behavior is a difficult subject matter, not because it [behavior] is inaccessible, but because it is extremely complex. Since it is a process, rather than a thing, it cannot be easily held still for observation" (Skinner, 1953, p. 15). This in part explains the predilection for demonstrable experimenter control of behavior (Sidman, 1960) in organizations and trading off sample size for extensive time-series data (Komaki & Goltz, 2001) among members of the OBM culture. Operant behavior is functionally defined as "behavior the properties of which can be modified by its effects on the environment. This class of behavior has also been called instrumental, and corresponds closely to the behavior colloquially referred to as voluntary" (Catania, 1968, p. 340). But radical behaviorists define behavior even more broadly as not only what a person does in an overt process, as noted above, but also what takes place within the individual, "such as thinking [an operant-like process], breathing [respondent behavior] or holding one's breath [operant-like process]" (Vargas, 2009, p. 337; see also Luthans & Kreitner, 1975, 1985).

OBM Perspectives on Theory Versus Data and Subjective Versus Objective Variables

Hopkins (1999) posed the following question and related strategy: "Is it time that we recognize our principles as an empirical theory, the collection of generalizations for our field" (p. 68). He went on to suggest how OBM should carefully relate its principles with reports regarding interventions based on them by way of insuring that others in the "scientific community" will agree that our principles do constitute an "empirical theory" (Hopkins, 1999, p. 68). This is not a rhetorical question, idle musing, or "interesting" intellectual exercise. Rather, how shall the OBM culture express a grand theory to differentiate it from IOP's "inside story" (i.e., $B_C = f(P_C, E_C)$)?

If OBM's theories and methods are related to a single (and singular) figure, and de facto, Father of behavior analysis, that individual would be B. F. Skinner (1931, 1950, 1953, 1956, 1957, 1938/1966, 1966a, 1966b, 1969; 1971, 1981). But, in OBM's "outside story" approach to improving human behavior, members of the OBM culture have looked to applied behavior analysis (ABA; Baer et al., 1968) for guidance (Daniels, 1977), where Jack Michael has been recognized (Dickinson, 2000) as the Father of OBM based, in part, on his work with Ayllon (Ayllon & Michael, 1959). Bill Hopkins' (1999) remarks are consistent with Skinner's early thinking. This is evident in Skinner's (1938/1966) reflections that appear in the preface to the seventh printing of *The Behavior of Organisms*. Here he succinctly explains and parsimoniously describes the role played by A in his 1931 behavioral expression: $R = f(S,A)$ where R was a response, S a stimulus, and with A, in his own words, he "was arguing that rate of eating [R], or of pressing a lever [R] when pressing was reinforced with food, was to be described as a function of a 'third variable'—that is, a variable in addition to stimulus and response, in this case a *history of deprivation and satiation* [emphasis added]" (p. x). He also intended elements of A to be "a convenient way of referring to *environmental* variables" (p. x). Here I treat this variable as a way of capturing a wide array of factors that can account for different behavior in the presence of apparently similar environmental conditions or contingencies.

For obvious reasons, the following changes to Skinner's expression are adopted for present, and, hopefully, future purposes. $B = f(S,H)$, where B is any observable or otherwise reliably recordable operant and/or respondent behavior that replaces R. A, third variables, is replaced with H, historical and/or events contemporaneous with and systematically related to B in the context of S, environmental stimuli as antecedents, consequences and/or correlates of B. Thus, H is essentially any history with objective three-term contingencies of reinforcement or recent history of deprivation/satiation relative to operant/respondent behavior that, when known by the behavior analyst or OBM intervention designer, helps account for observed behavior and suggests ways to better manage B and accomplishments that depend on B.

For example, OBM researchers successfully predicted differing patterns of simulated investment decisions during extinction preceded by a history with variable schedules of investment decision outcomes (Goltz, 1992; Hantula & Crowell, 1994). Their results provide convincing demonstrations of the role reinforcement history plays in individuals' subsequent behavior. The pattern of participants' investments (grouped and not individual data) during extinction following a history of winnings from a "partial reinforcement" schedule conformed roughly with what is called the *partial reinforcement extinction effect* (PREE; Capaldi, 1966), evidenced by a rise and eventually decline in amounts invested per trial. (For other related perspectives on this phenomenon see Bragger, Hantula, Bragger, Kiman, & Kutcher [2003] and Brecher & Hantula [2005].)

We know that operant and respondent behavior processes are, in practice, more or less confounded, particularly outside the laboratory (cf. Cherrington et al. [1971] and Scott & Podsakoff [1985]). For example, accepting an award or receiving negative performance feedback or job loss may include simple or complex operants accompanied by respondents manifest as emotional feelings called happiness or anger, embarrassment or shame, or other respondents that accompany these occasions, making the contribution of each intractable *outside the laboratory* (Brown & Herrnstein, 1975; Hutchinson, 1977; Mackintosh, 1977; Olson, Laraway, & Austin, 2001; Schwartz & Gamzu, 1977; Scott & Podsakoff, 1985; Weiss, 1990). They may all be made objectively measurable, albeit not precisely, outside controlled laboratory conditions, unless the contingency analyst adopts an approach developed by Mechner (2008a, 2008b). So the S component of OBM's behavior equation can be subscripted to reflect that the same stimulus may be an antecedent and consequence of a behavior, $_aS_c$, that elicits respondents in conjunction with evoking operants. For example, a cup of Starbucks coffee evokes my picking it up and drinking it, while at the same time I am sensing and enjoying its aroma prior to and while taking my first sip. Scott and Podsakoff (1985) provide a relatively thorough rendering of these complexities as they apply to motivation, leadership, and management.

The S functions as a discriminative stimulus or Ess Dee ($_aS \equiv S^D$) indicating an opportunity for access to a reinforcer (B → C = a reinforcer) or an

Ess Delta ($_aS \equiv S^\Delta$) extinction (absence of access to reinforcements or onset of extinction (B → ∅)) of the preceding behavior. For an $_aS$ or S_c to function as an S^D and an S_c to function as a reinforcer, S_c^+, or punisher, S_c^-, among adults, typically depends critically on the behavioral history of the person, H, including events in the relatively distant past (cf. Baum [2005] and Vroom [1964]). Antecedents that function as S^Ds may do so only in the context of or following specific establishing operations or EOs (Olson, et al., 2001) or motivating operations or MOs (Laraway, Snycerski, Michael, & Poling., 2003), if their effects as antecedents and consequences are temporally pinpointed so they conform with applications of the *contiguity-based law of effect* (Skinner, 1966b). But the physical location of history H, according to Skinner (1966b) consists of "changes in the responding . . . [individual]" (p. 12). Most readers find that some reinforcing experiences, even if in one's remote history, may evoke and account for some occasions of their own behavior repeatedly for the remainder of their lives, fade with the passage of time, or are altered by subsequent experiences. For example, individuals may choose to undergo treatment aimed at eliminating enduring or lingering effects of historical events, such as behavioral therapies to eliminate or reduce phobic responses.

If we continue to use *tried and true principles* (OBM's empirical theory, Hopkins [1999]), we may recognize that the matching law can be accommodated by our grand theory. For example B = f(matching law, H), although H is typically held constant in basic research animal studies. For present purposes, in a simple two-alternative choice environment, the matching law can be reduced to the following equation: $B_1/B_2 = V_1/V_2$, where Bs are rates of each of two behaviors and Vs are rates of reinforcement "value" correlated with their respective Bs. It is reasonable to expect that the Vs will function as measures of satisfying consequences or positive reinforcers, dissatisfying aversive consequences (punishers), or amalgams of the two types of consequences. Rachlin (1982) has recognized that the matching law can be derived from the laws of behavioral economics. Thus, roughly speaking, individuals can be expected to attempt to or to *actually maximize* $V_1 + V_2$ subject to constraints (Mawhinney, 1982). This provides a point of contact with Vroom's (1964) V-I-E theory in that both V-I-E and the matching law predict maximization of choices among concurrent schedules of reinforcement. Although it remains to be directly replicated, I have reported an unequivocal occasion of a human maximizing reinforcements received by creating and following reinforcement maximizing switching rules in the context of concurrent FR (count-based fixed ratio) VI (time and behavior-based variable interval) schedules of reinforcement (Mawhinney, 1982).

One of the more generally, if only tacitly, recognized principles of behavior routinely used in OBM field research (cf. Kerr, 1975) is Baum's (1973) *correlation-based law of effect* which states that "behavior increases in frequency if the increase is correlated with an increase in rate of reinforcement or a decrease in rate of aversive stimulation" (p. 145). While we have not explored every principle encompassed by our empirical theory of behavior, members of the OBM community should be familiar with the majority of them. And members of the IOP community should be familiar with those that are less technical but widely recognized, e.g., reinforcement (positive/negative), punishment (positive/negative), extinction, shaping, differential reinforcement of other behavior (DRO), modeling, and the Premack Principle (1965), to name a few. We have reviewed the theories underpinning these principles and the grand theory that encompasses virtually all of them (but see Garcia & Koelling, 1966).

TO BORROW OR BUILD AN OBM THEORY OF JOB SATISFACTION?

The IOP perspective on JS was covered in some detail above. Aguinis' (2010) *organizational responsibility* (OR) is defined as "context specific organizational actions and policies that take into account stakeholders' expectations and the triple bottom line of economic, social and environmental performance" (p. 858). Practices arising from or congruent with OR in the IOP culture are fairly similar in terms of their functions compared to dimensions of Wolf's (1978) concept of Social Validity (SV). But Schwartz and Baer's (1991) critical exposition proposes an SV concept somewhat narrower in scope than IOP's OR concept. Even more narrow, but closely related conceptually to IOP's approach to JS and JP relationships, is Parson's (1998) suggestion that service employees also be considered customers or consumers of OBM interventions as management practices in the spirit of the Schwartz and Baer (1991) perspective on service delivery personnel. While Schwartz and Baer (1991) write of simple survey/questionnaire methods used to assess satisfaction among consumers with SV practices in relatively negative terms, Parson's (1998) review of service system employee reactions to OBM methods per se found consumer support for this form of assessment, in most cases. It is worth noting that JS has been and continues to be an IOP focus of attention since at least 1917 (Thorndike, 1917). The IOP culture has a long history of, de facto, treating organizational personnel as a population of consumers to whom they indirectly provide a service, with heightened *employer awareness* of and *sensitivity to* the role of JS in JP. While it is tempting to assume OBM interventions improve or maintain participants' JS, I have indicated why this could be an unfounded assumption (Mawhinney, 1984, 1989). Suffice it to say, some members of the OBM culture share the IOP culture's concern for developing organizational practices that facilitate employee JS and effective and efficient JP.

The OR construct(s) in the IOP culture "does not seem to be a topic that receives much attention in the literature of mainstream I/O psychology, or even psychology in general" (Aguinis, 2010, p. 855). The reason may appear in Aguinis' (2010) definition of OR "as *context-specific organizational actions and policies that take into account stakeholders' expectations and the triple bottom line of economic, social, and environmental performance* [emphasis added]." (p. 858). Assessing an organization's performance on any one of these dimensions is no small task, let alone assessing performance on all of them. On the other hand, Wolf (1978) *pinpointed*, if a bit broadly, the behavior among members of ABA and, de facto today, the OBM culture as well, what would be classified as contributing to social validity of members' behavior and *accomplishments*:

> 1. The social significance of the *goals*. Are the specific behavioral goals really what society wants? 2. The social appropriateness of the *procedures*. Do the ends justify the means? *That is, do the participants, caregivers and other consumers consider the treatment procedures acceptable?* [emphasis added] 3. The social importance of the *effects*. Are *consumers satisfied* [emphasis added] with the results? *All* the results, including any unpredicted ones? (p. 207)

Given the diversity among our customers, it is reasonable to conclude that we should use a contingency approach to assessing SV of our interventions and design client-specific or standardized practices or systems depending on client or customer needs. For models in our literature see the following: Ludwig and Geller (2000), McSween (2003), Wolf, Kirigin, Fixsen, Blase, and Braukmann, (1995). This, of course, begs the question, "Who are our customers?" (Schwartz & Baer, 1991). Within organizations, who we and our customers are depends upon whom and where individuals are situated in the FO system.

We could be outside contractors and/or academic researchers. But we could be FO leaders, managers, supervisors and/or members of the OBM culture who have surmised from Wolf's (1978) clarion call that FOs have internal customers in their first-line workers, staff, or service delivery personnel, as well as clients they serve (Schwartz & Baer, 1991). This insight, that members of FOs are also customers, was recognized and acted upon by members of the OBM culture working *with* them. Parsons (1998) reviewed the OBM literature regarding what, in the IOP culture, would be called *job satisfaction* and, in the human services sector of OBM (Reid, 1998), may be called *consumer satisfaction and/or procedural acceptability*. This concept is usually examined among staff in terms of acceptability and/or enjoyment of treatment procedures and work assignments. There does not seem to be a well-validated and generally applicable tool for identifying, *a priori*, consequences that are highly likely to function as positive reinforcers for use in short-term interventions and long term standard operating procedures or practices; promising exceptions are procedures described by Daniels (1989), and job analyses and description practices suggested by Komaki and Minnich (2001). These procedures are widely used among workers in public service and private for-profit organizations.

Attempting to classify a priori "positive" or "satisfying" contingencies of reinforcement in a work setting should contribute to measurable job satisfaction among participants. Therefore, socially validated practices, of which accurate identification of positive reinforcers may become a part (cf. Wilder, Therrien, & Wine, 2006), should yield increased job satisfaction among organizational members. But based on field experiences, Daniels (1989) recognized and alerted supervisors, managers, and leaders to the fact that what function as reinforcing consequences can and do vary through time. This may be one explanation of the Wilder, Rost, and McMahon (2007) finding that managers are not highly reliable predictors of consequences that function as reinforcers among those whose behavior they are charged with managing. In fact, it is also possible to administer reinforcers among work group members in ways unexpectedly "perceived" to be unfair and consequently reduce both performance and job satisfaction among group members (cf. DeNisi, 2011). A type of tacit unfairness and unintended feedback occurs when, for example, performance appraisal "systems" fail to take into consideration and address issues such as specifying results or outcomes that are beyond the control of the individual(s) whose behavior is assessed. This problem has been assessed and a remedy recommended by Komaki and Minnich (2001). Their approach probably qualifies as an IOP/OBM hybrid approach to job analysis and performance appraisal. As to the numbers, Bucklin, Alvero, Dickinson, Austin, and Jackson (2000) found IOP scored "Quite impressively, . . . , social validity was assessed in 51% of the field studies (29 of 57)" (p. 59); citing Nolan, Jarema, & Austin (1999), JOBM's score was about half that at 27%. Worse, from 1998 to 2009 the mean number of SVs reported for OBM studies fell to "mean = 20%; $n = 17$" according to VanStelle et al. (in press).

A related issue clearly implicated by the matching law is negative effects of delayed positive reinforcer deliveries on reinforcement value, grossly stated as $V = A/1 + D$, where A is amount of a reinforcer and D is delay between occasions of B and receipt of A (Rachlin, 1989). While this may seem obvious, experience suggests managers overlook this, and we should not take such issues for granted even in a laboratory setting (cf. Rao & Mawhinney, 1991). Reid and Parsons (1996) verified this fact among participants in a training program, albeit not with respect to the quantitative matching law. Given the nature of interventions in human service systems, whether to develop an OBM theory of job satisfaction is moot. Hopkins' (1999) characterization of our empirical theory leads us to recognize that in an implicit or tacit theory of job satisfaction in our behavior principles and practices, positive reinforcement is associated with feelings of "joy" (Skinner, 1974). Moreover, the following laws of behavior are sources of principles that belong to our behavioral theory: (a) the law of relative effect or matching law (Herrnstein, 1970); (b) the correlation based law of effect (Baum, 1973); (c) reinforcement value maximization in the context of the matching relation (Mawhinney, 1982); and d) behavioral economics (Green, Kagel, & Battalio, 1982; Hursh, 1984). These are molar theories and therefore do not require that a consequence be virtually contiguous with behavior to effect its reinforcement. And they suggest cumulative effects of reinforcers (punishers) contingent on performances will account for variations in performance-related behavior and satisfaction. Reporting gross relations among applications of our empirical theory and JS as an element of SV can and should become standard practices where possible.

However, general and situation-specific verbal protocols, including rating scales and choice-based assessments of procedural acceptability, are sorely needed (cf. Wolf, 1978). Attractiveness (valence?) or reinforcement value of consequences and choice-based preference assessments imply a reduction in aversiveness or increase in satisfaction of work-related procedures. Members of the OBM culture, due to their reinforcement histories, are prone to directly attack problems of this ilk, socially validating effects of OBM on "quality of work life." Green, Reid, Passante, and Canipe (2008) described and validated efficacy of a behavior change strategy that involved "Changing Less-Preferred Duties to More-Preferred."

OBM research provides a stellar example of a difference between IOP and OBM traditions and strategies. To its credit, IOP has long been concerned with building sources of job satisfaction into jobs' P × E relations per se and recognizing that there is a job-person fit issue, e.g., the well-recognized interaction between job characteristics, E_c, and job incumbent, P_c (e.g., growth need strength) by fitting jobs to people (Hackman & Oldman, 1980) and vice-versa via selection and placement practices (Hackman & Oldman, 1980; Loher, Noe, Moeller, & Fitzgerald, 1985). However, this writer finds emerging OBM traditions that effectively fit people to jobs *by changing both* (Green et al., 2008) highly attractive, whether "one-shot" and using highly specialized assessment instruments or more standardized and validated instruments (cf. DeNisi, 2011). These variations describe innovations from which some will be selected based on their utility to improve the lives of others. The OBM culture has encouraged implementation of large-scale organization change and/or development programs and assessed their effects on members' job satisfaction (Hopkins, 1995, 1996). But Abernathy (1996) might raise the issue of pay equity, and this issue needs research.

OBM SMALL-SCALE AND ORGANIZATION-WIDE DEVELOPMENT USING IOP JOB SATISFACTION ASSESSMENT TECHNOLOGIES

Wilk and Redmon (1990) published a study in which goal setting was adjusted on a daily basis, while overtime and absenteeism served as surrogates of productivity. Absenteeism rose coincident with onset of their intervention. This was believed to reflect JS, at least in part, but because JS was not otherwise assessed there was no way to know whether the "blip" in absenteeism was due to it. Subsequent research on goal setting and feedback was designed to increase productivity *and JS* (Wilk & Redmon, 1997). Job satisfaction was measured with an IOP-type measure, the *Work Environment Scale* (*WES*) (Moos, 1981). All facets ($N = 10$) of the JS measure improved as a result of the intervention. "Most importantly, task clarity and supervisor support were reported as greatly improved (more than two standard deviations), while work pressure was reported to have been reduced (one standard deviation)" (Wilk & Redmon, 1997, p. 60). The first two dimensions are job satisfaction facets that should reflect the greatest impact from this intervention, but reduced work pressure is also important. Role ambiguity is typically aversive and increases stress (Glowinskowski & Cooper, 1986) accompanied by physical symptoms correlated with job dissatisfaction (Schleicher et al. 2010, p. 153, mean $\rho = -0.22$) among role occupants. OBM practitioners are well-prepared to deal with these issues and should consider creating SV and/or IOP methods of JS assessment.

In a 2008 invited address to members of the Association for Behavior Analysis (ABA) entitled "Meaningful Change at the Cultural Level: Behavioral Systems Revisited," Bill Redmon critiqued OBM's penchant for small-scale organizational change. He described a system he created as Manager of Leadership and Development at The Bechtel Group. Asked whether he was still using JS systems to establish social validity (Wolf, 1978) and organizational member development and assessment, Bill said,

> Every Senior Vice President who runs a business or manages an organization is accountable for action planning to address gaps in employee satisfaction. . . . I monitor Satisfaction with Immediate Supervisor which has moved from a neutral zone to a strength over the 5 years that we have been doing upward feedback for our supervisors. (Bill Redmon, personal communication, September, 2010)

At Bechtel, job satisfaction measures are used diagnostically and as means of monitoring the practices among members in the sense of social validity, e.g., are results being achieved *in the right way?*

OBM/IOP HYBRID RESEARCH WITH IMPLICATIONS FOR JOB SATISFACTION

Filipkowski and Johnson (2008), on the other hand, were in no position to make important system level changes over many years as Redmon did at Bechtel. Rather, they capitalized on the opportunity afforded them by the closing of one plant within their focal organization's complex and geographically dispersed operations. This revealed differences between reactions among union and nonunion members. The differences were reflections of differences in their cultural practices (Mawhinney, 1992, 1995; Redmon & Mason, 2001) to the extent they could reasonably be inferred from the data presented. Filipkowski and Johnson (2008) assessed relations among three IOP attitude measures (P_cs), job insecurity, organizational commitment, and intentions to turnover; one OBM observation based measures of *on-task behavior* and two company metrics, plant productivity, and defective parts per million (DPPM) produced. Effects of an announced plant closing in another state had both expected and unexpected effects. *On-task behavior* among workers in a union plant rose, unexpectedly. As one would expect (due to ceiling effects), the behavior remained high in the one nonunion plant for which data were available. Levels of productivity in two nonunion plants were higher than for the one union plant for the two months prior to the plant closing announcement and remained steady the two months following the announcement, while productivity in the union plant fell, more than this writer would have expected, from between plus 15% to 20% to an ultimate low (during the study) of *minus* 10%. Baseline levels of DPPM for one nonunion plant remained at or below 500 DPPM and near zero for the other nonunion plant, and DPPM was near zero for both nonunion plants following the plant closing announcement. The monthly DPPMs during baseline for the union plant were as follows: 1500, 3000, 3500, 2500. The union plant postbaseline DPPMs were 2000 and about 2400. Unless there existed great differences in parts being produced or unreliability of their equipment, these data reflect a huge performance deficit in the union plant workers' performance before and after the announcement.

That organizational members' were confronted, de facto, with a Hobson's Choice is reflected in the job insecurity correlation with absenteeism ($r = .14$, ns) and in particular the job insecurity correlation with actual turnover (r of virtually zero). The job performance problems' correlation with absenteeism ($r = .26$, $p < .01$) is higher than the job insecurity correlation ($r = .14$); the latter is typically observed between job satisfaction and absenteeism and/or performance but with a different (negative) sign for performance (Schleicher et al., 2010, p. 153, Table 4.1).

The Schleicher et al. (2010) *Job Attitudes and Work Values* data will likely serve as a source of standards for comparison of survey results as diagnostics for some years into the future. For example, what is the *practical* significance of the organizational commitment by intention to turnover $r = -.45$ ($p < .01$) in the present study? When compared to the $r = -.47$ for an $N = 136{,}270$ individuals, it is found to be virtually equal to the average correlation reported among 351 studies (Schleicher et al., 2010, p. 159). Thus, while correlation data such as those reported by Filipkowski and Johnson may help us *understand* why organizational members adopt the formal and nonformal practices that they do (Mawhinney, 2009), they are more likely to be more useful for isolating problems arising from them when they are appreciably different from what has been established as "average" or "normal" correlations in a large number of other studies across a large number of other organizations. Even exceedingly low correlations can, however, prove useful when they point to confounding effects of Hobson's Choice on employees' behavior and verbal responses to survey instruments. Filipkowski and Johnson (2008) have "broken the ice," as it were, by demonstrating how combined IOP and OBM practices may yield more information about troubled work organizations than either might alone.

DISCUSSION AND CONCLUSIONS

The IOP and OBM cultures differ dramatically with respect to their grand theories that reflect the high value the IOP culture places on "understanding" people, P_c, as averages of constructs assessed via verbal reports rather than individual's objectively measured actions. There are few concrete objective anchors in these "nomological networks." Generally, OBM community members are not accustomed to accounting for on-the-job behavioral phenomena using the language and methods of IOP theorists/researchers. Those on-the-job phenomena that have been examined have typically found low correlations (Filipkowski & Johnson, 2008; cf. Schleicher et al., 2010; Smith, 1977). In the OBM culture, there is heavy reliance on demonstrated prediction and control of behavior as directly observed and counted as B, and not as B_c, where B_c would be questionnaire-based measures of *behavior or behavioral intention constructs*. Even the environment, E, with which behavior of P_c interacts, is yet another set of IOP constructs, or E_cs. These constructs, when arranged in models and nomological networks, are designed to provide *understanding* of "behavioral" phenomena. Performance is typically a function of real behavior of a performance rater that is converted via mediation of rating systems technologies into another construct (cf. DeNisi, 2011). This is subject to halo bias, demonstrated empirically by Thorndike (1920) in a 1915 study. Thus, with respect to job satisfaction, IOP reveals its preference for theory and perceptions of behavior constructs, B_c, over objective direct measures of behavior. Members of the OBM research culture prefer prediction and/or control of behavior per se or *accomplishments* (Gilbert, 1978) as tangible evidence of performance, e.g., units of work completed, sales volume, an/or a change in absence rates clearly attributable to a leader's actions (Luthans & Kreitner, 1985). For an important exception, see Pritchard, Jones, Roth, Stuebing, and Ekeberg (1988), from which members of the OBM culture might learn something about creating and assessing large scale interventions. As we learned from Bill Redmon, however, when those responsible for the SV of their organization that cascades down among members of its leadership team(s), desired consequences of leaders' behavior may well be B_c, resulting from members' scores on job satisfaction scales. And, with some unavoidable delay, followers' job satisfaction, B_c, may be an important, albeit, delayed consequence of a leader's "real" behavioral interactions with followers. For an early critique of the logic and practicality of this strategy, see O'Brien and Dickinson (1982).

The OBM culture should not eschew IOP practices associated with developing subjective measures of people or the world as experienced (H) from the consumers' perspective, but should consider caveats by Schwartz and Baer (1991). These practices should be recognized as serving two purposes among OBM members: (a) understanding people in the sense that IOP seeks to understand people so that we may communicate with members of other cultures also interested in improving SV of behavioral interventions and programs in FOs; and (b), continuing to support Hall's (1980) reminder that "the goal of the field of OBM is to establish a technology of broad-scale performance improvement and organizational change so that employees will be more productive and happy [Skinner, 1974], and so that our organizations and institutions will be more effective and efficient in achieving their goals" (p. 142). For a thorough discussion of "happiness" as a modern construct, see Stajkovic (2006). Creating productive, happy employees and goal-achieving organizations will benefit society. In keeping with the OBM culture's preference for "objectification" of "subjective" variables such as happiness and satisfaction, it behooves us to continue our efforts to socially validate (Schwartz & Baer, 1991; Wolf, 1978) all of our interventions and programs, be they small or large in scale, and whether they be ephemeral (Fellows & Mawhinney, 1997; Mawhinney & Fellows-Kubert, 1999) or sustained in the long term (Fox, Hopkins, & Anger, 1987; Sigurdsson, & Austin, 2006).

REFERENCES

Abernathy, W. B. (1996). *The sin of wages*. Memphis, TN: PerfSys Press.

Aguinis, H. (2010). Organizational responsibility: Doing good and doing well. In S. Zedeck (Ed.), *APA handbook of industrial and organizational psychology* (Vol. 3; pp. 855–879). Washington, DC: American Psychological Association.

Ayllon, T., & Michael, J. (1959). The psychiatric nurse as a behavioral engineer. *Journal of the Experimental Analysis of Behavior, 2*, 323–334.

Baer, D. M., Wolf. M. M., & Risley. T. R. (1968). Some current dimensions of applied behavior analysis. *Journal of Applied Behavior Analysis, 1*, 91–97.

Baum, W. M. (1973). The correlation-based law of effect. *Journal of the Experimental Analysis of Behavior, 20*, 137–153.

Baum, W. M. (2005). *Understanding behaviorism: Behavior, culture, and evolution* (2nd ed.). Malden, MA: Blackwell.

Beehr, T. A., Glaser, K. M., Canali, K. G., & Wallwey, D. A. (2001). Back to basics: Re-examination of demand-control theory of occupational stress. *Work & Stress, 15*, 115–130.

Beehr, T. A., Jex, S. M., & Ghosh, P. (2001). The management of occupational stress. In C. M. Johnson, W. K. Redmon, & T. C. Mawhinney (Eds.), *Handbook of organizational performance: Behavior analysis and management* (pp. 225–254). Binghamton, NY: Haworth.

Bowling, N. A., Beehr, T. A., Wagner, S. H., & Libkuman, T. M. (2005). Adaptation-level theory, opponent process theory, and dispositions: An integrated approach to the stability of job satisfaction. *Journal of Applied Psychology, 90*, 1044–1053.

Bragger, J. D., Hantula, D. A., Bragger, D., Kiman, J., & Kutcher, E. (2003). When success breeds failure: History, hysteresis, and delayed exit decisions. *Journal of Applied Psychology, 88*, 6–14.

Brecher, E. G., & Hantula, D. A., (2005). Equivocality and escalation: A replication and preliminary examination of frustration. *Journal of Applied Social Psychology, 35*, 2606–2619.

Brown, R., & Herrnstein, R. J. (1975). *Psychology*. Boston, MA: Little, Brown & Company.

Bucklin, B. R., Alvero, A. M., Dickinson, A. M., Austin, J., & Jackson, A. K. (2000). Industrial-Organizational Psychology and Organizational Behavior Management: An objective comparison. *Journal of Organizational Behavior Management, 20(2)*, 27–75.

Capaldi, E. J. (1966). Partial reinforcement: A hypothesis of sequential effects. *Psychological Review, 73*, 459–477.

Cascio, W., & Boudreau, J. (2008). *Investing in people*. Upper Saddle River, NJ: Pearson.

Catania, A. C. (1963). Concurrent performances: A baseline for the study of reinforcement magnitude. *Journal of the Experimental Analysis of Behavior, 6*, 299–300.

Catania, A. C. (1968). *Contemporary research if operant behavior*. Glenview, IL: Scott Foresman.

Cherrington, D. J., Reitz, H. J., & Scott, W. E. (1971). Effects of contingent and noncontingent reward on the relationship between satisfaction and task performance. *Journal of Applied Psychology, 55*, 531–536.

Cranny, C. J., Smith P. C., & Stone, E. F. (1992). *Job satisfaction: How people feel about their jobs and how it affects their performance*. New York, NY: Lexington.

Daniels, A. C. (1977). Editorial. *Journal of Organizational Behavior Management, 1(1)*, v–vii.

Daniels, A. C. (1989). *Performance management* (3rd ed.). Tucker, GA: Performance Management Publications.

DeNisi, A. S. (2011). Managing performance to change behavior. *Journal of Organizational Behavior Management, 31*, 262–276.

Dickinson, A. M. (2000). The historical roots of organizational behavior management in the private sector. *Journal of Organizational Behavior Management, 20(3)*, 9–58.

Diefendorff, J. M., & Chandler, M. M. (2010). Motivating employees. In S. Zedeck (Ed.), *APA handbook of industrial and organizational psychology* (Vol. 3; pp. 65–135). Washington, DC: American Psychological Association.

Dubin, R. (1976). Theory building in applied areas. In M. Dunnette (Ed.), *Handbook of industrial and organizational psychology* (pp. 17–39). Chicago, IL: Rand McNally.

Dunnette, M. D. (Ed.) (1976). Preface. *Handbook of industrial and organizational psychology*. Chicago, IL: Rand McNally.

Eberly, M. B., Holtom, B. C., Lee, T. W., & Mitchell, T. R. (2009). Control voluntary turnover by understanding its causes. In E. Locke (Ed.), *Handbook of principles of organization behavior* (2nd ed.; pp. 123–142). Chichester, England: Wiley.

Fellows, C., & Mawhinney, T. C. (1997). Improving telemarketers' performance in the short-run using operant concepts. *Journal of Business and Psychology*, *11*(4), 411–424.

Filipkowski, M., & Johnson, C. M. (2008). Comparisons of performance and job insecurity in union and nonunion sites of a manufacturing company. *Journal of Organizational Behavior Management*, *28*, 218–237.

Fox, D. K., Hopkins, B. L., & Anger, W. K. (1987). The long-term effects of a token economy on safety performance in open-pit mining. *Journal of Applied Behavior Analysis*, *20*, 215–224.

Garcia, J., & Koelling, R. A. (1966). Relation of cue to consequence in avoidance learning. *Psychonomic Science*, *4*, 123.

Gilbert, T. F. (1978). *Human competence: Engineering worthy performance*. New York, NY: McGraw-Hill.

Glenn, S. S. (1991). Contingencies and metacontingencies: Relations among behavioral, cultural, and biological evolution. In P. A. Lamal (Ed.), *Behavioral analysis of societies and cultural practices* (pp. 39–73). Washington, DC: Hemisphere.

Glowinskowski, S. P., & Cooper, C. L. (1986). Managers and professionals in business/industrial settings. *Journal of Organizational Behavior Management*, *28*(2), 90–109.

Goltz, S. M. (1992). A sequential learning analysis of decisions in organizations to escalate investments despite continuing costs or losses. *Journal of Applied Behavior Analysis*, *25*, 561–574.

Green, C. W., Reid, D. H., Passante, S. & Canipe, V. (2008). Changing less-preferred duties to more-preferred: A potential strategy for improving supervisor work enjoyment. *Journal of Organizational Behavior Management*, *28*, 90–109.

Green, L., Kagel, J. H., & Battalio, R. C. (1982). Ratio schedules of reinforcement and their relation to economic theories of labor supply. In M. L. Commons, R. J. Herrnstein, & H. Rachlin (Eds.), *Quantitative analyses of behavior: 2. Matching and maximizing accounts* (pp. 395–429). Cambridge, MA: Ballinger.

Hackman, J. R., & Oldham, G. R. (1980). *Work redesign*. Upper Saddle River, NJ: Pearson.

Hall, B. L. (1980). Editorial. *Journal of Organizational Behavior Management*, *2*(3), 145–150.

Hantula, D. A., & Crowell, C. R. (1994) Intermittent reinforcement and escalation processes in sequential decision making. *Journal of Organizational Behavior Management*, *14*(2), 7–36.

Hantula, D. A., & Kondash, J. (2007, May). *Job satisfaction: The management tool and responsibility revisited, or the case for affective measurement in OBM.* PowerPoint presentation at the Annual Meeting of Association for Behavior Analysis–International, San Diego, CA.

Hayes, S. C., Bond, F. W., & Barns-Holmes, D. (2006). *Acceptance and mindfulness at work: Applying acceptance and commitment therapy and relational frame theory to Organizational Behavior Management.* Binghamton, NY: Haworth.

Hopkins, B. L. (1995). An introduction to developing, maintaining, and improving large-scale, data-based programs. *Journal of Organizational Behavior Management, 15*(1/2), 7–10.

Hopkins, B. L. (1996). A continuation of the series on developing, maintaining, and improving large-scale, data-based programs. *Journal of Organizational Behavior Management, 16*(1), 1–2.

Hopkins, B. L. (1999). The principles of behavior as an empirical theory and the usefulness of that theory in addressing practical problems. *Journal of Organizational Behavior Management, 19*(3), 67–74.

Herrnstein. R. J. (1970). On the law of effect. *Journal of the Experimental Analysis of Behavior, 13*, 243–266.

House, R. J. (1971). A path-goal theory of leader effectiveness. *Administrative Science Quarterly, 16*, 321–339.

Hull, C. L. (1943). *Principles of behavior.* New York, NY: Appleton-Century.

Hull, C. L. (1951). *Essentials of behavior.* New Haven, CT: Yale University Press.

Hursh, S. R. (1984). Behavioral economics. *Journal of the Experimental Analysis of Behavior, 42*, 435–452.

Hutchinson, R. R. (1977). By-products of aversive control. In W. K. Honig & J. E. R. Staddon (Eds.), *Handbook of operant behavior* (pp. 415–431). Englewood Cliffs: NJ: Prentice-Hall.

Judge, T. A., & Klinger, R. (2009). Promote job satisfaction through mental challenge. In E. Locke (Ed.), *Handbook of principles of organization behavior* (2nd ed.; pp. 108–121). Chichester, England: Wiley.

Judge, R. A., Thoresen, C. J., Bono, J. E., & Patton, G. K. (2001). The job satisfaction-job performance relationship: A qualitative and quantitative review. *Psychological Bulletin, 127*, 376–407.

Kerr, S. (1975). On the folly of rewarding A, while hoping for B. *Academy of Management Journal, 18*, 769–782.

Komaki, J. L., & Goltz, S. M. (2001). Within-group research designs: Going beyond program evaluation. In C. M. Johnson, W. K. Redmon, & T. C. Mawhinney (Eds.), *Handbook of organizational performance: Behavior analysis and management* (pp. 81–137). Binghamton, NY: Haworth.

Komaki, J. L., & Minnich, M. R. (2001). Developing performance appraisals: Criteria for what and how performance is measured. In C. M. Johnson, W. K. Redmon, & T. C. Mawhinney (Eds.), *Handbook of organizational performance: Behavior analysis and management* (pp. 51–80). Binghamton, NY: Haworth.

Landy, F. J. (1978). An opponent process theory of job satisfaction. *Journal of Applied Psychology, 63*, 533–547.

Laraway, S., Snycerski, S. Michael, J., & Poling, A. (2003). Motivating operations and terms to describe them: Some further refinements. *Journal of Applied Behavior Analysis, 36*, 407–414.

Lawler, E. E., & Porter, L. W. (1967). The effect of performance on job satisfaction. *Industrial Relations, 7*, 20–28.

Lewin, K. (1935). A *dynamic theory of personality*. New York, NY: McGraw-Hill.

Lewin, K. (1938). *The conceptual representation and the measurement of psychological forces*. Part of the Contributions to Psychological Theory Series. Durham, NC: Duke University Press.

Locke, E. A., (1969). What is job satisfaction? *Organizational Behavior and Human Performance, 4*, 309–336.

Locke, E. A. (2009). Attain emotional control by understanding what emotions are. In E. Locke (Ed.), *Handbook of principles of organization behavior* (2nd ed.; pp.145–159). Chichester, UK: Wiley.

Locke, E. A., Smith, P. C., Kendall, L. M., Hulin, C. L., & Miller, A. M. (1964). Convergent and discriminant validity for areas and methods of rating satisfaction. *Journal of Applied Psychology, 48*, 313–319.

Loher B. T., Noe, R. A., Moeller, N. L., & Fitzgerald, M. P. (1985). A meta-analysis of the relation of job characteristics to job satisfaction. *Journal of Applied Psychology, 70*, 280–289.

Ludwig, T. D., & Geller, E. S. (2000). Intervening to improve the safety of occupational driving: A behavior-change model and review of empirical evidence. *Journal of Organizational Behavior Management, 19*(4), 1–124.

Luthans, F., & Kreitner, R. (1975). *Organizational behavior modification*. Glenview, IL: Scott Foresman.

Luthans, F., & Kreitner, R. (1985). *Organizational behavior modification and beyond*. Glenview, IL: Scott Foresman.

Mackintosh, N. J. (1977). Stimulus control: Attentional factors. In W. K. Honig, & J. E. R. Staddon (Eds.), *Handbook of operant behavior* (pp. 481–513). Englewood Cliffs, NJ: Prentice-Hall.

Malott, R. W. (1992). A theory of rule-governed behavior and organizational behavior management. *Journal of Organizational Behavior Management, 12*(2), 45–65.

Mawhinney, T. C. (1982). Maximizing versus matching in people versus pigeons. *Psychological Reports, 50*, 267–281.

Mawhinney, T. C. (1984). Philosophical and ethical aspects of organizational behavior management. *Journal of Organizational Behavior Management, 6*(1), 5–31.

Mawhinney, T. C. (1989). Job satisfaction as a management tool and responsibility. *Journal of Organizational Behavior Management, 10*(1), 187–192.

Mawhinney, T. C. (1992). Evolution of organizational cultures as selection by consequences: The Gaia hypothesis, metacontingencies, and organizational ecology. *Journal of Organizational Behavior Management, 12*(2), 1–26.

Mawhinney, T. C. (2001). Organization-environment systems as OBM intervention context: Minding your metacontingencies. In L. Hayes, J. Austin, & R. Houmanfar (Eds.), *Organizational change* (pp. 137–166). Reno, NV: Context Press.

Mawhinney, T. C. (2009). Identifying and extinguishing dysfunctional and deadly organizational practices. *Journal of Organizational Behavior Management, 29*(3), 231–256.

Mawhinney, T. C., & Fellows-Kubert, C. (1999). Positive contingencies versus quotas: Telemarketers exert countercontrol. *Journal of Organizational Behavior Management, 19*(2), 35–57.

McSween, T. E. (2003). *Values based safety process: Improving your safety culture with behavior-based safety.* Hoboken NJ: Wiley.

Mechner, F. (2008a). Behavioral contingency analysis. *Behavioral Processes, 78,* 124–144.

Mechner, F. (2008b). Applications of the language for codifying behavioral contingencies. Retrieved from http://mechnerfoundation.org/newsite/downloads.html

Miller, B. L. (1980). Editorial. *Journal of Organizational Behavior Management, 2*(3), 145–150.

Mitchell, T. R. (1974). Expectancy models of job satisfaction, occupational preference and effort: A theoretical, methodological and empirical appraisal. *Psychological Bulletin, 81,* 1053–1077.

Moos, R. H. (1981). *Work environment scale manual* (3rd ed.). Palo Alto, CA: Consulting Psychologists Press.

Nolan, T. V., Jarema, K. A., & Austin, J. (1999). An objective review of the *Journal of Organizational Behavior Management*: 1987–1997. *Journal of Organizational Behavior Management, 19*(3), 83–114.

O'Brien, R. M., & Dickinson, A. M. (1982). Introduction to industrial behavior modification. In R. M. O'Brien, A. Dickinson, & M. Rosow (Eds.), *Industrial behavior modification* (pp. 7–34). New York, NY: Pergamon.

Olson, R., Laraway, S., & Austin, J. (2001). Unconditioned and conditioned establishing operations in organizational behavior management. *Journal of Organizational Behavior Management, 21*(2), 7–35.

Organ, D. W., Podsakoff, P. M., & McKenzie, S. B. (2006). *Organizational citizenship behavior.* Thousand Oaks, CA: Sage.

Parsons, M. B. (1998). A review of procedural acceptability in organizational behavior management. *Journal of Organizational Behavior Management, 18*(2), 173–190.

Pinder, C. C. (2008). *Work motivation in organizational behavior* (2nd ed.) New York, NY: Psychology Press.

Porter, L. W., & Lawler, E. F., III. (1968). *Managerial attitudes and performance.* Homewood, IL: Irwin-Dorsey.

Premack, D. (1965). Reinforcement theory. In D. Levine (Ed.), *Nebraska Symposium on Motivation, 13,* 123–180. Lincoln, NE: University of Nebraska Press.

Pritchard, R. D., Jones, S. D., Roth, P. L., Stuebing, K. K., & Ekeberg, S. E. (1988). Effects of group feedback, goal setting, and incentives on organizational productivity. *Journal of Applied Psychology Monograph, 73*(2), 337–358.

Rachlin, H. (1982). Economics of the matching law. In M. L. Commons, R. J. Herrnstein, & H. Rachlin (Eds.), *Quantitative analyses of behavior: Vol. 2. Matching and maximizing accounts* (pp. 347–374). Cambridge, MA: Ballinger.

Rachlin, H. (1989). *Judgment, decision and choice.* New York, NY: W. H. Freeman.

Rao, R. K., & Mawhinney, T. C. (1991). Superior-subordinate dyads: Dependence of leader effectiveness on mutual reinforcement contingencies. *Journal of the Experimental Analysis of Behavior, 56,* 105–118.

Redmon, W. K., & Agnew, J. L. (1991). Organizational behavioral analysis in the United States: A view from the private sector. In P. A. Lamal (Ed.), *Behavior analysis of societies and cultural practices* (pp. 125–139). Washington, DC: Hemisphere.

Redmon, W. K., & Mason, M. A. (2001). Organizational culture and behavior systems analysis. In C. M. Johnson, W. K., Redmon, & T. C. Mawhinney (Eds.), *Handbook of organizational performance: Behavior analysis and management* (pp. 437–456). Binghamton, NY: Haworth.

Redmon, W. K., & Wilk, L. A. (1991). Organizational behavioral analysis in the United States: Public sector organizations. In P. A. Lamal (Ed.), *Behavior analysis of societies and cultural practices* (pp. 107–123). Washington, DC: Hemisphere.

Reid, D. H. (1998). *Organizational behavior management and developmental disabilities services: Accomplishments and future directions*. Binghamton, NY: Haworth.

Reid, D. H., & Parsons, M. B. (1996). A comparison of staff acceptability of immediate versus delayed verbal feedback in staff training. *Journal of Organizational Behavior Management, 16*(2), 35–47.

Riketta, M. R. (2008). The causal relations between job attitudes and performance: A meta-analysis of panel studies. *Journal of Applied Psychology, 93*, 472–481.

Robinson, J. P., Athanasiou, R., & Head, K. B. (1969). *Measures of occupational attitudes and occupational characteristics*. Ann Arbor, MI: Institute for Social Research.

Rosenberg, M. J., & Hoveland, C. I. (1960). Cognitive, affective, and behavioral components of attitude. In M. Rosenberg, C. Hoveland, W. McGuire, R. Abelson, & J. Brehm (Eds.). *Attitude organization and change*. New Haven: CT: Yale University Press.

Rosseau, D. (2009). Preface. In E. Locke (Ed.), *Handbook of principles of organization behavior* (2nd ed.; pp. xv–xxiii). Chichester, UK: Wiley.

Schleicher, D. J., Hansen, D., & Fox, K. E. (2010). Job attitudes and work values. In S. Zedeck (Ed.), *APA handbook of industrial and organizational psychology* (Vol. 3; pp. 137–189). Washington, DC: American Psychological Association.

Schwartz, I. S., & Baer, D. M. (1991) Social validity assessments: Is current practice state of the art? *Journal of Applied Behavior Analysis, 24*, 189–204.

Schwartz, B., & Gamzu, E. (1977). Pavlovian control of operant behavior. In W. K. Honig & J. E. R. Staddon (Eds.), *Handbook of operant behavior* (pp. 53–97). Englewood Cliffs: NJ: Prentice-Hall.

Scott, W. E., & Podsakoff, P. M. (1985). *Behavioral principles in the practice of management*. New York, NY: Wiley.

Sidman, M. (1960). *Tactics of scientific research*. New York, NY: Basic Books.

Sigurdsson, S. O., & Austin, J. (2006). Institutionalization and response maintenance in organizational behavior management. *Journal of Organizational Behavior Management, 24*(4), 41–75.

Skinner, B. F. (1931). The concept of the reflex in the description of behavior. *Journal of General Psychology, 5*, 427–458.

Skinner, B. F. (1938/1966, 7th printing). *The behavior of organisms*. New York, NY: Appleton-Century-Crofts.

Skinner, B. F. (1950). Are theories of learning necessary? *Psychological Review, 57*, 193–216.
Skinner, B. F. (1953). *Science and human behavior*. New York, NY: Free Press.
Skinner, B. F. (1956). A case history in scientific method. *American Psychologist, 11*, 221–233.
Skinner, B. F. (1957). *Verbal behavior*. New York, NY: Appleton-Century-Crofts.
Skinner, B. F. (1966a). What is the experimental analysis of behavior? *Journal of the Experimental Analysis of Behavior, 9*, 213–218.
Skinner, B. F. (1966b). Operant behavior. In W. Honig (Ed.), *Operant behavior: Areas of research and application* (pp. 12–32). New York, NY: Appleton-Century-Crofts.
Skinner, B. F. (1969). *Contingencies of reinforcement: A theoretical analysis*. New York, NY: Appleton-Century-Crofts.
Skinner, B. F. (1971). *Beyond freedom and dignity*. New York, NY: Knopf.
Skinner, B. F. (1974). *About behaviorism*. New York, NY: Knopf.
Skinner, B. F. (1981). Selection by consequences. *Science, 213*, 501–504.
Smith, F. J. (1977). Work attitudes as predictors of attendance on a specific day. *Journal of Applied Psychology, 62*, 16–19.
Smith, P. C. (1967). The development of a method of measuring job satisfaction. In E. Fleishman (Ed.), *Studies in personnel and industrial psychology* (Rev. ed.; pp. 343–350). Homewood, IL: Dorsey.
Stajkovic, A. D. (2006). Development of a core confidence–higher order construct. *Journal of Applied Psychology, 91*(6), 1208–1224.
Starr, M. K. (1971). *Management: A modern approach*. New York, NY: Harcourt Brace Jovanovich.
Stone-Romero, E. F. (2010). Research strategies in Industrial and Organizational Psychology: Nonexperimental, quasi-experimental, and randomized experimental research in special purpose and non-special purpose settings. In S. Zedeck (Ed.), *APA handbook of industrial and organizational psychology* (Vol. 1; pp. 37–72). Washington, DC: American Psychological Association.
Thorndike, E. L. (1917). The curve of work and the curve of satisfyingness. *Journal of Applied Psychology, 1*, 265–267.
Thorndike, E. L. (1920). A constant error in psychological ratings. *Journal of Applied Psychology, 4*, 25–29.
Tolman, E. L. (1932). *Purposive behavior in animals and men*. New York, NY: Century.
VanStelle, S. E., Vicars, S. M., Harr, V., Miguel, C. F., Koerber, J. L., Kazbour, R. & Austin, J. (in press). The publication history of the *Journal of Organizational Behavior Management*: An objective review and analysis: 1998–2009. *Journal of Organizational Behavior Management*.
Vargas, J. S. (2009). *Behavior analysis for effective teaching*. New York, NY: Routledge.
Vroom, V. H. (1964). *Work and motivation*. New York, NY: Wiley.
Weiss, H. M. (1990). Learning theory and industrial and organizational psychology. In M. D. Dunnette & L. M. Hough (Eds.), *Handbook of industrial and organizational psychology* (Vol. 1; pp. 171–221). Palo Alto, CA: Consulting Psychologists Press.

Wertheimer, M. (1972). *Fundamental issues in psychology*. New York, NY: Holt, Rinehart & Winston.

Wilder, D. A., Rost, K., & McMahon, M. (2007) The accuracy of managerial prediction of employee preference. *Journal of Organizational Behavior Management*, 27(2), 1–14.

Wilder, D. A., Therrien, K., & Wine, B. (2006). A comparison between survey and verbal choice methods of identifying potential reinforcers among employees. *Journal of Organizational Behavior Management*, 25(4), 1–13.

Wilk, L. A., & Redmon, W. K. (1990). A daily-adjusted goal-setting and feedback procedure for improving productivity in a university admissions department. *Journal of Organizational Behavior Management*, 11(1), 55–75.

Wilk, L. A., & Redmon, W. K. (1997) The effects of feedback and goal setting on the productivity and satisfaction of university admissions staff. *Journal of Organizational Behavior Management*, 18(1), 45–68.

Wolf, M. M. (1978). Social validity: The case for subjective measurement or how applied behavior analysis is finding its heart. *Journal of Applied Behavior Analysis, 11*, 203–214.

Wolf, M. M., Kirigin, K. A., Fixsen, D. L., Blase, K. A., & Braukmann, C. J. (1995). The Teaching-Family Model: A case study in data-based program development and refinement (and dragon wrestling). *Journal of Organizational Behavior Management*, 15(1/2), 11–68.

Zedeck, S. (2010). Introduction. In S. Zedeck (Ed.), *APA handbook of industrial and organizational psychology* (Vol. 1; pp. xxi–xxxiv). Washington, DC: American Psychological Association.

From Job Analysis to Performance Management: A Synergistic Rapprochement to Organizational Effectiveness

CHARLES R. CROWELL
University of Notre Dame, Notre Dame, Indiana, USA

DONALD A. HANTULA
Temple University, Philadelphia, Pennsylvania, USA

KARI L. McARTHUR
Hillsdale College, Hillsdale, Michigan, USA

This article shows how OBM research and practice can incorporate tools from IOP to achieve an effective and socially valid organizational improvement strategy. After a brief review of both fields, a project is described in a major domestic corporation illustrating a synthesis of OBM and IOP techniques. Value-added repair service was targeted for change in a major manufacturer of large home appliances. To accomplish these goals, a standard IOP job analysis was used to define the critical service behaviors related to the value-added dimension, and then both a selection system as well as a customer-directed behavioral assessment instrument to measure this service were developed and validated. Finally, an OBM intervention using task clarification, feedback, and praise was employed to improve the behaviors targeted by the behavioral assessment tool. A synopsis of the results is presented, along with some practical and theoretical implications of this rapprochement of IOP and OBM.

This special issue explores the question of how best to characterize the relationship between Organizational Behavior Management (OBM) and Industrial and Organizational Psychology (IOP). A better understanding of this relationship may lend itself to more effective strategies for creating synergies between these fields. Both fields have long shared the common goal of improving organizational effectiveness (Lawshe, Dunlap, Kahn, Shartle, & Katzell, 1959; Luthans & Kreitner, 1975), but each employs distinctively different research methods toward that end (Bucklin, Alvero, Dickinson, Austin, & Jackson, 2000). A very practical reason to create such synergies is to improve the overall quality of organizational research (Geller, 2003a, 2003b) to produce better ways to improve organizational effectiveness. Our goal in this article is to show how OBM research can incorporate certain tools from IOP, thereby achieving a more effective and socially valid organizational improvement strategy. We will illustrate our own particular marriage of OBM and IOP by describing a project conducted in a major domestic service-oriented company. Before presenting the details of this work, we will first compare several general characteristics of both fields.

A SELECTIVE COMPARISON OF IOP AND OBM

OBM and IOP share common roots. Both descended from the functionalist school of experimental psychology and share notable forefathers, including E. L. Thorndike and J. B. Watson. Indeed Watson started one of the first doctoral programs in IOP at Johns Hopkins and was one of the founders of the Psychological Corporation (DiClemente & Hantula, 2000; Lowman, Kantor, & Perloff, 2007). Despite common ancestors, these independent traditions evolved separately and have led to distinctly different empirical and theoretical approaches to their shared goal of organizational improvement. Detailed analyses of these historical differences have been provided elsewhere (Bucklin et al., 2000; Dickinson, 2000; Katzell & Austin, 1992), and so our comparisons here will be highly selective.

Key Features of IOP

Two early influences on the development of IOP are most germane to the present comparison. One was the emergence of "individual differences" measures of mental capacities, traits, and abilities (Bucklin et al., 2000), a trend based on the assumption that many important causal influences on human behavior arose from covert or internal states. As a result, special measurement techniques (e.g., intelligence or personality tests) and statistical procedures (e.g., factor analysis) were necessary to reveal these inherently unobservable constructs. The Hawthorne studies were a second important influence (Katzell & Austin, 1992). These studies were of historical importance in seeming to show that work performance can vary systematically as a result of different extrinsic (e.g., illumination, wages) or social (e.g., supervision, team development) characteristics of the work environment. However, it should be noted that this traditional interpretation of the Hawthorne results has been called into question by subsequent analyses showing that the so-called "Hawthorne Effect" may in fact be attributable to the effects of feedback and reinforcement, commonly used OBM interventions (Parsons, 1992).

These early influences left IOP with a legacy affecting the ways in which research is conducted. For example, a large percentage of published IOP studies use self-report questionnaires or other types of test instruments administered to a group of individuals to see how the presumed psychological factors or attitudes measured by those instruments relate to one another or to measures of work performance (Bucklin et al., 2000). A correlational research strategy employing psychological tests or attitude surveys as primary data collection tools is a common approach in IOP research, as are between-groups designs that compare dependent measures across separate groups exposed to different work-related environmental, social, or educational conditions. Likewise, the common use of sophisticated psychometric and statistical methods in this field further attests to the importance placed on measurement of covert states, traits, and processes. Given these historical emphases in IOP, it is perhaps not surprising that many in this field regard overt behavior more as a proxy for inward and psychologically relevant causal factors than as an end in itself, a somewhat ironic stance given that most proponents of IOP probably would agree with OBM researchers that employee behavior ultimately produces organizational outcomes.

Also, it seems fairly clear historically that IOP has been more science- than practice-oriented (Bucklin et al., 2000; Katzell & Austin, 1992), a divide that continues to inspire debate (Silzer, Erickson, & Cober 2010). Nonetheless, IOP has produced a number of practical contributions, including three techniques that are especially relevant to the work we will describe below: job analysis, personnel selection, and satisfaction assessment. Job analysis is the examination of a particular job to understand what specific tasks and responsibilities are involved, as well as what knowledge, skills, and abilities (KSAs) are required to perform that job. Personnel selection builds on a job analysis to assess a prospective job candidate's KSAs in relation to what is required for that job. Satisfaction assessment involves measuring perceptions and attitudes toward the job (Mawhinney, 2011).

Key Features of OBM

In contrast to IOP, OBM grew out of the behavior analysis movement in psychology (Dickinson, 2000). The most commonly acknowledged historical influence on OBM is the work of B. F. Skinner, especially his principle of "selection by consequences" (Bucklin et al., 2000). Skinner's extensive laboratory investigations of reinforcement contingencies (e.g., Ferster & Skinner, 1957), along with his vast theoretical extrapolations to the human arena (e.g., Skinner, 1953, 1971), firmly established an organism's reinforcement history as a prime element in understanding its behavior. In addition, considerable work in the behavior analytic tradition has demonstrated the importance of antecedent conditions in the prediction and control of behavior (DiClemente & Hantula, 2003). Within this tradition, "control" is demonstrated for individual subjects by showing that one or more targeted behaviors can be changed through the systematic application or removal of specific antecedents or consequences. Bucklin et al. (2000) note that published OBM studies are characterized by (a) overt behavioral rather than covert internal targets, (b) use of "within-subject" research designs to demonstrate behavioral control over time, and (c) interventions based on the systematic introduction of antecedents or consequences.

The legacy of behavior analysis for OBM research has been significant. For the most part, OBM researchers approach the goal of organizational improvement by targeting and changing behaviors that influence or give rise to key success-related outcomes thereby focusing on work behavior itself, rather than on internal states of workers (Crowell & Anderson, 1982a, 1982b). From the beginning, OBM has been largely a practical rather than a theory-testing endeavor (Bucklin et al. 2000), although theory testing is important in OBM research (e.g., Goltz, 1999; Hantula & Crowell, 1994). The field's applied focus clearly concerns creating and documenting techniques and tools that organizations can use to improve their own efficiency and effectiveness (Crowell & Anderson, 1982a). Among the important products of this effort is the development of performance analysis diagnostic tools for identifying where important improvement opportunities exist within organizations (e.g., Diener, McGee & Miguel, 2009; Mager & Pipe, 1997), together with the refinement of effective behavior change interventions based on the application of certain kinds of antecedents (e.g., goal setting, task clarification) or consequences (e.g., feedback, reinforcement).

A BEGINNING RAPPROCHEMENT: THREE KEY ELEMENTS

Neither IOP nor OBM has a corner on the organizational improvement market. Despite theoretical and methodological differences in these fields, each one has produced useful perspectives and tools for addressing different pieces of the organizational improvement puzzle. For example, job analysis and personnel selection methods are effective tools for understanding work tasks and getting the right people doing the job. Likewise, satisfaction assessment methods are useful for understanding the personal impact of work procedures and environments on the quality of work life. By the same token, identifying the right behavioral targets and deploying effective interventions to create improvement is another key element of a total organizational change strategy. We believe the overarching important goal of enhancing an organization's success, which undoubtedly influences its culture and affects the lives of its many stakeholders (e.g., employees, managers, customers, investors), trumps any historical or academic differences that may have separated IOP and OBM. Moreover, as others already have suggested (Bucklin, 2000; Geller, 2003a), a rapprochement of these fields can and should occur, at least at a practical level. We set out to do just that with the beginning effort described below.

A service context was particularly well-suited to our rapprochement of IOP and OBM. Two features of the service industry stand out in this regard. One is the special role of behavior in this industry. In most if not all service settings, behavior can be both the means of production as well as the end product. Unlike manufacturing or other industries where tangible commodities are involved, service usually involves a provider saying or doing something for a recipient or consumer in what has been described as either a "help me" or "fix it" capacity (Albrecht & Zemke, 1985). This feature makes the service industry a natural context to implement OBM-style performance change strategies focusing directly on provider behaviors.

A second salient feature of service settings involves what has been called the "value added" dimension; service behaviors add value when they positively impact the quality of life in some way, such as when a service provider goes "the extra mile" on behalf of a service recipient (Albrecht & Zemke, 1985). In IOP, this value added element often is labeled "organizational citizenship behavior" (Organ, Podsakoff, & MacKenzie, 2006) and is measured with some type of questionnaire. Moreover, many service settings can be sufficiently complex and challenging (O'Hara, Johnson, & Beehr, 1985) so as to behoove organizations to use careful job analysis and employee selection procedures as part of their efforts to establish an effective "service culture."

The elements we summarize here incorporate these approaches into a hybrid OBM-IOP methodology. Some of this work is reported in more detail by McArthur, Hantula, and Crowell (2011). The setting for this work was a service branch of a major manufacturer of large home appliances. The organization's strategic plan was to expand its national factory service branches rapidly and significantly, so as to increase revenue by in-sourcing repair services rather than reimbursing subcontractors; and to build brand loyalty and repeat sales within its existing customer base. To help the organization achieve these objectives, the researchers embarked on a two-pronged approach to enhance the in-house repair function of the organization. One prong involved a strategy to hire the best service technicians (STs), while the second prong involved a performance management system to ensure that

STs regularly delivered the desired service behaviors. Both prongs depended importantly on a careful analysis of the job of an ST.

Job Analysis and Employee Selection: Springboards for Performance Improvement

JOB ANALYSIS

A thorough job analysis of the service technician position was conducted from three perspectives (branch managers, service technicians, customers). This analysis included (a) observations of STs' visits occurring in customer's homes; (b) interviews with STs and their managers; (c) analysis of task inventory questionnaires completed by STs and managers; (d) post-service interviews with customers; (e) analyses of critical incidents supplied by STs, their managers, and customers; and (f) information gathered from six customer focus groups conducted across the country. The job analysis identified 23 specific "value-added" behaviors of STs that were believed by the company to be highly relevant to the consumer's "quality of life" in connection with the service visit.

A BEHAVIORAL SELECTION SYSTEM FOR STs

The job analysis data led to KSA and task inventories, which were then translated into a selection system following the procedures outlined by Delery, Wright, McArthur, and Anderson (1994). This system assessed applicants on each of six key job dimensions (customer relations, administration, diagnosis, repair, technical/professional improvement, and sales). The selection system included (a) a structured interview presenting *behavioral description interview questions* intended to assess an applicant's background, work history, experiences, and goals through the use of general/broad type of interview questions, as well as *situational interview questions* designed to assess an applicant's knowledge, skills, abilities, and reactions to work situations through the use of specific types of interview questions, each with benchmarked responses; (b) a behaviorally driven, situational roleplay wherein the applicant demonstrated a complete service call, including customer interaction, problem diagnosis of an actual appliance, call documentation, and monetary transaction; and (c) a battery of five written tests to assess cognitive ability and technical aptitude.

A concurrent validation study (Delery et al., 1994) found that the selection system was a valid predictor of supervisor performance ratings of the service technicians. Accordingly, an extensive training protocol was established to ensure the validated selection system was appropriately and consistently applied across the organization; before being authorized to utilize the selection system, all users were required to complete a behaviorally based, self-paced training program that included postassessment. The training program included an educational component, practice in interpreting potential interviewee responses, and applying associated benchmarks of each interview question, along with role-play criteria using specially created video tapes of mock interviews.

Using Customer Perceptions to Measure VA Behaviors in Service Technicians

Once STs were in place, a system was needed to verify and maintain their delivery of desired service behaviors. All STs were dispatched into the field to repair customer appliances based on calls to an in-house service phone center. Accordingly, it was necessary to develop and evaluate a system to track the service provided by STs who worked off company premises in consumer residences. The company was concerned primarily about value added (VA) rather than help me (HM) service behaviors. Overall customer perceptions of the service visit were related importantly to the VA behaviors and HM behaviors related mainly to the repair itself, so adequate procedures already were in place to track this activity.

Assessment Instrument

A behavioral customer observation questionnaire (COQ) was created to assess customer perceptions of the 23 "value-added" behaviors during the service visit, along with several aspects of the customers' overall "satisfaction" with the visit. The "value-added" behavior assessment items on the COQ pertained to such matters as whether or not the ST provided an initial greeting, a demonstration of the repaired product, and a business card. The "satisfaction" items pertained to such matters as whether or not the customer would call this company for service again, want the same technician back, and recommend this company to a friend or family member. The "value-added" items were asked in a binary "yes/no" format, while the "satisfaction" items had a third "maybe" response choice. Management assigned each COQ item a point value based on the perceived importance of the ST behavior or the customer satisfaction dimension assessed by that item. Total points summed across all "yes" items for the COQ completed by a particular customer was the ST's measure of "value-added" service for that service visit.

COQ Return Rate Optimization

Different incentive conditions and distribution plans to increase COQ returns were compared. The three different incentive conditions were (a) a small gift mailed to the customer upon the receipt of a completed COQ, or (b) entry into a drawing for a kitchen appliance valued at over $300, or (c) no tangible incentive, only a promise the COQ would be used to improve future services. The two separate COQ distribution procedures consisted of (a) advance mailing to the customer after gaining permission by phone (less than 1% denied permission) so that it would arrive on the day preceding the service visit, or (b) handing to the consumer by the ST at the beginning of the service call. The small gift was generally more effective than either the drawing or the no incentive condition. Mailing the COQs resulted in markedly higher return rates (62%) than did handing them out (40%). Use of a gift resulted in a 19% improvement in return rate over no incentive for mailed questionnaires, whereas the improvement was 11% for those handed out by the ST. But with a drawing, the same improvement in return rate (6%) was produced by both distribution methods compared to the no incentive conditions.

COQ VERIFICATION

A trained observer, represented to the customer as a member of the office staff being cross-trained, occasionally accompanied STs on their service calls on 46 randomly chosen days. Unbeknownst to the ST or the customer, the observer covertly completed a separate COQ based on the VA behaviors exhibited by the ST. Across all 46 joint visits, the observer-customer agreement percentage for VA items on the COQ was 83%.

Improving VA Service and Customer Satisfaction: Targeting COQ Scores With OBM Procedures

Using the COQ as the primary method for tracking VA service behaviors, OBM procedures were used to improve the VA service of 14 STs in a Midwestern metropolitan area.

VA SERVICE AND CUSTOMER SATISFACTION

Individual COQ scores were derived from the 23 VA behaviors assessed. These point scores out of 100 were expressed as percentages and were averaged weekly for each ST to yield a *customer relations* score. To uphold the reliability and accuracy of these scores, occasional joint visits of a trained observer continued throughout this study. Also, ongoing checks were made to insure that the STs were distributing a COQ form to each customer and not selectively distributing forms just to individuals who they believed would respond favorably.

OBM PROCEDURES

An 11-week baseline period, during which COQs were mailed to customers, began the study. Sequential introduction of four separate interventions followed, consisting respectively of 6 weeks of technician distribution (TD) of COQs, 8 weeks of task clarification (TC), 10 weeks of feedback (FB), and 7 weeks of social praise (SP). These interventions were deployed across three separate matched groups in a time-staggered fashion. Interventions were withdrawn for all groups after the last week of praise. The protocols for these various interventions generally followed those established by Crowell, Anderson, Abel, & Sergio (1988). In this protocol, task clarification was delivered in a group meeting using a memo outlining the specific desired behaviors (see Crowell et al., 1988).

Feedback consisted of charts distributed to the STs displaying their mean customer relations scores across weeks, along with other measures. All of the graphs were coded to ensure ST anonymity. Each ST also received a weekly document that displayed the average points received for each of the 23 COQ questions for the forms returned the previous week and the average total customer relations score for the previous week. Also, each ST received a reduced-size version of every other ST's chart. All STs acknowledged their receipt of this weekly feedback in writing. In addition to these written materials, feedback also entailed verbal acknowledgement of each ST's most recent completion and COQ scores as displayed on the performance chart. This feedback was strictly non-evaluative, as described by Crowell et al. (1988), and occurred via a phone conversation between each ST and either the branch manager or another designated feedback provider.

The praise intervention maintained all aspects of the feedback intervention and also included the delivery of praise to those STs who showed weekly improvements in their feedback measures and/or maintained good performance. All praise was given during the weekly phone calls initiated during the feedback intervention.

The withdrawal stage was executed by indicating to all STs that the program would be "temporarily" put on hold. During this phase, STs did not receive any of the weekly performance feedback materials, but were asked to continue to "do their best" as well as to distribute their remaining supply of COQs. Data collection continued during this return to baseline period for six consecutive weeks.

Key Findings

COQs were left with the intended customer more than 87% of the time, and response rates were above 43% for the 8,152 COQ forms distributed for this study. Reliability of COQ observations remained high (>81% interrater agreement) over the course of 96 random checks throughout the study.

Figure 1 presents the mean customer relations score (indicative of VA service) by intervention collapsed over the three groups. The difference between what were essentially two "baseline" conditions involving the direct mailing of COQs to the customer (Baseline phase) and the handing of COQ

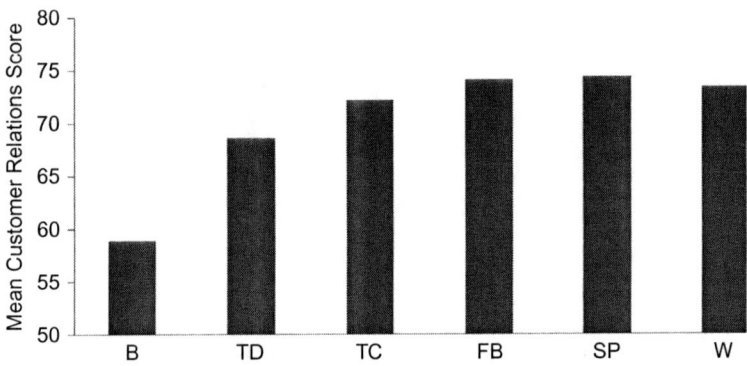

FIGURE 1 The mean Customer Relations Score averaged across weeks within interventions.

to the customer by STs (TD phase) was significant. Even so, however, the task clarification intervention (TC phase) was associated with a significant increase in VA service over the TD stage. Succeeding interventions, Feedback (FB) and Social Praise (SP), produced further increases, but these improvements were not significantly different from TC performance levels. Moreover, the observed decrease in VA service during the short withdrawal stage was not a significant drop off in this measure from the FB or SP phases.

Figure 2 shows intervention averages for the percentages of "yes" responses given to each of the three customer satisfaction questions on the COQ, averaged across technicians and groups. The first and third questions asked about perceptions related to the company (i.e., would you call this company again, or refer this company to someone), while the second question asked about the ST (i.e., would you want this person back). Figure 2 shows a somewhat different pattern across interventions for the latter item than for the former items. Each succeeding intervention seemed to have a positive incremental effect on customer satisfaction for the ST-related question, but not for the company related items, with a clear decrease in each during the withdrawal.

DISCUSSION

Both IOP and OBM methods were synthesized successfully to develop and evaluate a selection system, job performance criteria, and interventions to change ST behaviors and increase customer satisfaction. The IOP methods included job analysis, selection, focus-groups, and COQ development. OBM methods incorporated two behaviorally differentiated classes of service behaviors: (Help me vs. Value-added) and interventions that combined both antecedent (COQ Distribution and Task Clarification) and consequent effects (Feedback and Praise). Together, these methods produced a significant improvement in customer satisfaction with ST visits, along with heightened

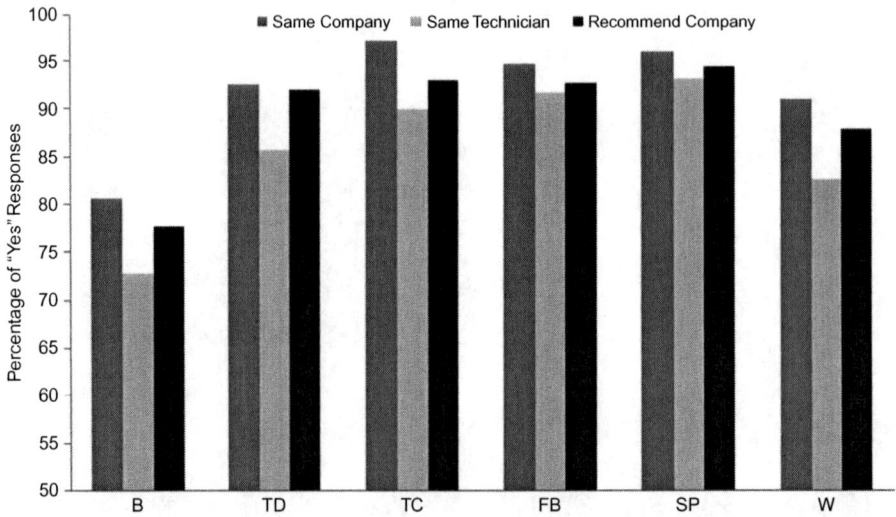

FIGURE 2 The mean percentage of "yes" responses averaged across technicians and weeks within interventions for each of the three customer satisfaction questions on the Customer Observations Questionnaire (COQ). Question 1: "If you needed to call for service again, would you call this same company?" Question 2: "If you needed to call for service again, would you call the same technician to service your appliance?" Question 3: "Would you recommend this same company to a friend or relative?"

customer perceptions of the company, a somewhat novel index of organizational effectiveness for OBM, but common in IOP. Not only were IOP and OBM interventions combined, but techniques typical of both camps also were employed to yield one approach to a methodological rapprochement of IOP and OBM.

It should be noted how these results speak to the relative effectiveness of IOP and OBM components in contributing to the overall performance improvement obtained with this hybrid methodology. Techniques like job analysis and selection are "springboards," as we described them. As any competitive diver knows, it's not the springboard itself, but rather how it is used that makes all the difference in the dive. Job analysis and selection are elements of a change strategy akin to "establishing operations" in behavior analysis. Accordingly, it is difficult to separate out the unique contributions these springboards make possible in an overall organizational improvement strategy.

Another way to look at our particular variant of an IOP and OBM synthesis is in terms of the age-old structure vs. function distinction. IOP techniques such as job analysis and selection may be viewed as structural inasmuch as they define the scope of a job, thereby bringing more (behavioral) clarity to the work and helping to insure people will have the KSAs necessary to do the job. But, structural interventions alone are not usually sufficient to initiate and sustain high levels of job performance. This is because giving employees more knowledge about their work from a job analysis does not automatically mean they will actually do the job differently. Moreover, selection accounts for 25% of work performance, at best (Schmidt & Hunter, 1998). The mere existence of KSAs on the job does not guarantee their use.

OBM interventions are largely functional. Task clarification prompts specific behaviors, while feedback, praise, and other reinforcement procedures provide consequences that may have both directing (S^D) as well as strengthening (S^R) effects on job behavior. However, reinforcing the wrong behaviors soon will lead to organizational ineffectiveness. Furthermore, all the reinforcement in the world does not bestow needed KSAs on someone who does not have them. Thus, structural and functional contributions can be synergistic in their effects on improving organizational effectiveness.

It is axiomatic within OBM that behavior is a function of its consequences. Timely consequences matter most to individuals. For example, Yankelovich and Immerwhar (1984) suggested that workers may be willing to trade pay for recognition and self-esteem in the workplace. OBM studies have demonstrated how to make poor performers better, if not excellent, to the point where the (formerly) worst performers become indistinguishable from the best (Anderson et al., 1982; Nicol & Hantula, 2005). But, function (behavior) must exist within a structure, and employees with the necessary KSAs may be more likely to perform well and thus may require less intensive OBM interventions than those without. Clearly, finding such individuals a priori can avoid the frustrating and wasteful a posteriori process of identifying and developing or removing those who lack the necessary KSAs.

Changes in the way work is conducted may eventually lead to a transformation in the role of selection techniques. The idea of "hiring for the organization, not the job" (Chatman, 1991) has much intuitive appeal as work becomes more organization-centric and less job-centric. The "organization" is the structure that contains reinforcers; perhaps the next challenge in selection is to identify prevailing sources of reinforcement and then find individuals whose preferences match the available reinforcers.

Problems and Solutions

Both IOP and OBM are devoted to application at some level and thus share certain common challenges and conceptual conundrums. IOP has sometimes been criticized for a lack of theory and theoretically-driven research (Hulin, 2002; Lefkowitz, 2010). This criticism suggests that predominantly application-driven research hinders intellectual advancement, which is a scientific concern. But, on the other hand, practitioner concerns are less conceptual and more pragmatic; that is, if an IOP technique works, then delineating the presumed theoretical underpinnings is a luxury, not a necessity. Similarly, OBM is has been criticized about theory, either for clinging to the theoretical basis of behavior analysis or for its apparent disavowal of theory altogether. It should be noted, however, that the latter critique is based largely on a misunderstanding of the intellectual humor contained in the title of Skinner's well-known 1950 paper on learning theories (the reality is this article was not a jeremiad against theory as much as a poke at those contemporaries who were preoccupied with it). And like IOP, OBM appears vulnerable to the criticism that its researchers ignore the theoretical foundations of interventions in favor of an emphasis on changing behavior in the workplace.

These circumstances point to a unique opportunity for another type of rapprochement between IOP and OBM: namely, uniting against a common enemy, one that regards both fields as academic facades for refining techniques, tools, and tricks to manipulate workers into increased productivity. As the present hybrid methodology example illustrates, IOP and OBM easily are synthesized at a practical, operational level (indeed a glance at Web sites from leading OBM-based consulting firms bears this out). The bigger challenge here is rapprochement at a conceptual and theoretical level.

One way to address this challenge is for OBM to become a subset of a larger IOP. Perhaps this is already occurring to some extent since OBM and related topics (i.e., "reinforcement theory," "organizational behavior modification") now are included in IOP encyclopediae and handbooks, and since OBM now is discussed (often in a fair way) in leading IOP textbooks (e.g., Aamodt, 2010). In this rapprochement, OBM's strength would be technical and methodological with successful applications and interventions. OBM techniques can become experimental tools for IOP researchers who want to "push constructs around" or systematically alter the work environment so as to manipulate theoretical constructs. OBM research tactics will augment the methodological tools of IOP; the attendant greater focus on measuring and recording behavior will facilitate work in job analysis, performance appraisal, and selection, where OBM may help to provide a solution to "the criterion problem" (Austin & Villanova, 1992; Farr, & Jacobs, 2006). Also, single subject designs may help move IOP research and application into small business settings, a growing part of the economy that has been largely neglected by IOP researchers due to its inherently small populations, but that is easily explored using OBM research methods (e.g., Milligan & Hantula, 2005). Theoretically, in this scenario, OBM would be more aligned with the "O" rather than "I" side of IOP, most likely subsumed under "work motivation." Unfortunately, other IOP topics such as leadership (e.g., Komaki,1998; Mawhinney, 2005) and decision making (e.g., Bragger et al., 2003) that also have been approached from an OBM perspective may not be as well represented within IOP if a behavioral perspective is constrained to the subtopic of "motivation," thereby quite possibly minimizing the theoretical contributions of this perspective.

Another rapprochement possibility for uniting against a common "enemy" would be for OBM to become the theory base for IOP. OBM, and its allied discipline of behavior analysis, provides a systematic, scalable way to understand all behavior in organizations. But, to do this, OBM would have to embrace the challenges inherent in IOP research and adopt IOP methods as needed. Under this option, IOP research and practice would need to shift to a much more behavioral focus, and IOP researchers would need to commit to behavioral constructs and, therefore, either reinterpret traditional IOP explanatory mechanisms in a more behavioral way, or abandon those mechanisms altogether. A good example of the former would be Parson's (1992) behavioral reanalysis of the fabled Hawthorne studies. The latter is exemplified by the more theoretically based OBM work of Bragger et al. (2003), or by a movement that would bring Acceptance and Commitment Therapy (ACT) and Relational Frame Theory (RFT), which handles private events and other constructs of interest in IOP, to bear on OBM (as suggested in the recent JOBM special issue edited by Steve Hayes). The good news here is that some subareas of IOP, like job analysis and training and development, already are very behavioral. However, for others like selection, a more radical shift would be required.

In any case, both OBM and IOP will need to become less dogmatic and more open to one another's influences. In some instances this has already happened, as evidenced by OBM journals that have published research using decidedly IOP methods, and IOP journals that have published research that is clearly behavioral. From a relativistic perspective on science (Feyerabend, 1975), no one theoretical stance is truth's sole proprietor; instead different stances can serve as foils for the other, illuminating relative strengths and weaknesses in each other. Of course, when the ultimate truth criterion for science is pragmatic, and that pragmatism is focused on organizational effectiveness (the common goal of IOP and OBM), theoretical differences should take a back seat to what actually works. As the present project clearly illustrates, both IOP and OBM methods can work harmoniously side by side—perhaps it is time for proponents of these two fields to find a way to follow suit.

REFERENCES

Albrecht, K., & Zemke, R. (1985). *Service America! Doing business in the new economy*. Homewood, IL: Dow Jones-Irwin.

Aamodt, M. G. (2010). *Industrial/Organizational Psychology*. Florence, KY: Cengage Learning.

Anderson, D. C., Crowell, C. R., Sponsel, S. S., Clark, M., & Brence, J. (1982). Behavior management in the public accommodations industry: A three-project demonstration. *Journal of Organizational Behavior Management*, 4(1/2), 33–66.

Austin, J., & Villanova, P. (1992). The criterion problem: 1917–1992. *Journal of Applied Psychology, 77*, 836–874.

Bragger, J. L., Hantula, D. A., Bragger, D., Kirnan, J., & Kutcher, E. (2003). When success breeds failure: History, hysteresis, and delayed exit decisions. *Journal of Applied Psychology, 88*, 6–14.

Bucklin, B. R., Alvero, A. M., Dickinson, A. M., Austin, J., & Jackson, A. K. (2000). Industrial-Organizational Psychology and Organizational Behavior Management. *Journal of Organizational Behavior Management, 20*(2), 27–75.

Chatman, J. A. (1991) Matching people and organizations: Selecting and socialization in public accounting firms. *Administrative Science Quarterly, 36*, 459–484.

Crowell, C. R., & Anderson, D. C. (1982a). The scientific and methodological basis of a systematic approach to human behavior management. *Journal of Organizational Behavior Management, 4*(1/2), 1–32.

Crowell, C. R., & Anderson, D. C. (1982b). Systematic behavior management: General program considerations. *Journal of Organizational Behavior Management, 4*(1/2), 129–163.

Crowell, C. R., Anderson, D. C., Abel, D., & Sergio, J. (1988). Task clarification, performance feedback, and social praise: Procedures for improving the customer service of bank tellers. *Journal of Applied Behavior Analysis, 21*, 65–71.

Delery, J. E., Wright, P. M., McArthur, K., & Anderson, D. C. (1994). Cognitive ability tests and the situational interview: A test of incremental validity. *International Journal of Selection and Assessment, 2*(1), 53–58.

DiClemente, D., & Hantula, D. A. (2000). John Broadus Watson: I/O psychologist. *The Industrial-Organizational Psychologist, 37*(4), 47–55.

DiClemente, D., & Hantula, D. A. (2003). Applied behavioral economics and consumer choice. *Journal of Economic Psychology, 24*, 589–602.

Diener, L., McGee, H., & Miguel, C. (2009). An integrated approach for conducting a behavioral systems analysis. *Journal of Organizational Behavior Management, 29*, 108–135.

Dickinson, A. M. (2000) The historical roots of Organizational Behavior Management in the private sector, *Journal of Organizational Behavior Management, 20*(3/4), 9–58.

Farr, J., & Jacobs, R. (2006). Unifying perspectives: The criterion problem today and into the 21st Century. W. Bennett, C. Lance, and D. Woehr (Eds.), P*erformance measurement: Current perspectives and future challenges* (pp. 321–337). Mahwah, NJ: Erlbaum.

Ferster, C. B., & Skinner, B. F. (1957). *Schedules of reinforcement.* Englewood Cliffs, NJ: Prentice-Hall.

Feyerabend, P. (1975). *Against method.* London, England: New Left Books.

Geller, E. S. (2003a). Should Organizational Behavior Management expand its content? *Journal of Organizational Behavior Management, 22*(2), 13–30.

Geller, E. S. (2003b). Organizational Behavior Management and Industrial/Organizational Psychology. *Journal of Organizational Behavior Management, 22*(2), 111–130.

Goltz, S. (1999). Can't stop on a dime: The roles of matching and momentum in persistence of commitment. *Journal of Organizational Behavior Management, 19*(1), 37–63.

Hantula, D. A., & Crowell, C. R. (1994). Intermittent reinforcement and escalation processes in sequential decision making: A replication and theoretical analysis. *Journal of Organizational Behavior Management, 14*(2), 7–36.

Hulin, C. L. (2002). Lessons from Industrial and Organizational Psychology. In J. M. Brett & F. Drasgow (Eds.), *The psychology of work: Theoretically based empirical research* (pp. 3–22). Mahwah, NJ: Erlbaum.

Katzell, R. A., & Austin, J. T. (1992). From then to now: The development of industrial-organizational psychology in the United States. *Journal of Applied Psychology, 77*, 803–835.

Komaki, J. L. (1998). *Leadership from an operant perspective.* New York, NY: Routledge.

Lawshe, C., Dunlap, J., Kahn, R., Shartle, C., & Katzell, R. (1959). Blueprinting the next ten years of industrial psychology: A symposium. *Personnel Psychology, 12*, 29–48.

Lefkowitz, J. (2010). Industrial-Organizational Psychology's recurring identity crises: It's a values issue! *Industrial and Organizational Psychology, 3*, 293–299.

Lowman, R. L., Kantor, J., & Perloff, R. (2007). A history of I-O psychology educational programs in the United States. In L. L. Koopes (Ed.), *Historical perspectives in Industrial and Organizational Psychology* (pp. 111–137). Mahwah, NJ: Erlbaum.

Luthans, F., & Kreitner, R. (1975). *Organizational behavior modification.* Glenview, IL: Scott Foresman.

Mager, R. & Pipe, P. (1997). *Analyzing performance problems: Or, you really oughta wanna—how to figure out why people aren't doing what they should be, and what to do about it* (3rd ed.). Atlanta, GA: Center for Effective Performance.

Mawhinney, T. C. (2005). Effective leadership in superior-subordinate dyads: Theory and data. *Journal of Organizational Behavior Management, 25*(4), 37–79.

Mawhinney, T. C. (2011). Job satisfaction: I/O Psychology and Organizational Behavior Management perspectives. *Journal of Organizational Behavior Management, 31*, 288–315.

McArthur, K., Hantula, D. A., & Crowell, C. R. (2011). *Improving the in-home repair service provided by a major home appliance manufacturer using a novel customer-based metric.* Manuscript submitted for publication.

Milligan, J., & Hantula, D. A. (2005). A prompting procedure for increasing sales in a small pet store. *Journal of Organizational Behavior Management, 25*(3), 37–44.

Nicol, N., & Hantula, D. A. (2001). Decreasing delivery drivers' departure times. *Journal of Organizational Behavior Management, 21*(4), 105–116.

O'Hara, K., Johnson, C. M., & Beehr, T. A. (1985). Organizational behavior management in the private sector: A review of empirical research and recommendations for further investigation. *Academy of Management Review, 40*(4), 848–864.

Organ, D. W., Podsakoff, P. M., & Mackenzie, S. B. (2006). *Organizational citizenship behavior: Its nature, antecedents, and consequences.* Beverly Hill, CA: Sage.

Parsons, H. (1992). Hawthorne: An early OBM experiment. *Journal of Organizational Behavior Management, 12*(1), 27–43.

Schmidt, F. L, & Hunter J. E. (1998). The validity and utility of selection methods in personnel psychology: Practical and theoretical implications of 85 years of research findings. *Psychological Bulletin, 124*, 262–274.

Silzer, R. F., Erickson, A. R., & Cober, R. T. (2010). Practice perspectives: Practitioner cohort differences: Different career stages or changing views? *The Industrial-Organizational Psychologist, 47*(3), 93–108.

Skinner, B. F. (1953). *Science and human behavior*. New York, NY: Free Press.

Skinner, B. F. (1971). *Beyond freedom and dignity*. New York, NY: Knopf.

Yankelovich, D., & Immerwahr, J. (1984). Putting the work ethic to work. *Society, 21*(2), 58–76.

A Tale of Two Paradigms: The Impact of Psychological Capital and Reinforcing Feedback on Problem Solving and Innovation

FRED LUTHANS
University of Nebraska–Lincoln, Lincoln, Nebraska, USA

CAROLYN M. YOUSSEF
Bellevue University, Bellevue, Nebraska, USA

SHANNON L. RAWSKI
University of Arkansas, Fayetteville, Arkansas, USA

This study drew from two distinct paradigms: the social cognitively based emerging field of positive organizational behavior or POB and the more established behaviorally based area of organizational behavior modification or OB Mod. The intent was to show that both can contribute to complex challenges facing today's organizations. Using a quasi-experimental research design (N = 1,526 working adults), in general both the recently recognized core construct of psychological capital (representing POB) and reinforcing feedback (representing OB Mod), especially when partially mediated through a mastery-oriented mindset, were positively related to problem solving performance, reported innovation, and subsequent psychological capital. The implications for theoretical understanding and practice conclude the article.

Managing employee behavior has always been at the forefront of organizational research and practice. Behavioral management and modification have been pursued in psychological research for almost a century (Bandura, 1969;

Pavlov, 1927; Skinner, 1938; Thorndike, 1913). Applied to organizational settings, Luthans (1973) developed and refined this behavioral paradigm into a five-step model of organizational behavior modification, or simply called OB Mod (Luthans & Kreitner, 1975, 1985). This OB Mod model provided a useful and effective framework for both research and application in order to identify, measure, analyze, contingently intervene in, and evaluate employees' performance-related behaviors. Research on this model in a wide range of organizational settings has clearly demonstrated a significant impact on performance improvement (See Stajkovic & Luthans, 1997 for a comprehensive review and meta-analysis and also see published studies over the years such as Luthans, Fox, & Davis, 1991; Luthans, Paul, & Baker, 1981; Luthans, Rhee, Luthans, & Avey, 2008; Peterson & Luthans, 2006; Stajkovic & Luthans, 2001, 2003).

In addition to this established research from the OB Mod approach coming from the behavioral paradigm, in this study we also draw from the emerging research in positive organizational behavior (POB) mainly coming from a distinctively different social cognitive paradigm (Luthans, 2002a, 2002b; Luthans & Avolio, 2009; Luthans & Youssef, 2007; Wright, 2003). Specifically, using positivity as the commonality and unifying theme in both paradigms, our purpose is to first develop theory-driven hypotheses and then empirically test through a quasi-experimental research design the impact of positive psychological capital or simply PsyCap (drawn from POB, see Luthans & Youssef, 2004; Luthans, Youssef, & Avolio, 2007) and positive contingent feedback (drawn from OB Mod) on employee problem solving performance, reported innovation, and subsequent positivity (i.e., PsyCap). Furthermore, PsyCap and contingent feedback drawn from their respective paradigms are conceptualized and integrated into an overall positive model shown in Figure 1. As shown, the PsyCap serves as a cueing mechanism, and the feedback a reinforcing mechanism for a unique mediating process of a mastery-oriented mindset, which in turn facilitates problem solving and reported innovation. We also proposed that these mechanisms may lead to an upward spiral of subsequent positivity.

FIGURE 1 An integrated positivity model of two paradigms for problem solving and innovation.

POSITIVE ORGANIZATIONAL BEHAVIOR AND PSYCHOLOGICAL CAPITAL

Using the field of positive psychology (Seligman & Csikszentmihalyi, 2000; Snyder & Lopez, 2002) as a point of departure for application to the workplace, Luthans coined the term *positive organizational behavior*, or simply POB, and defined this new paradigm in OB as "the study and application of positively oriented human resource strengths and psychological capacities that can be measured, developed, and effectively managed for performance improvement in today's workplace" (Luthans, 2002b, p. 59). Emerging out of this field of POB has been what Luthans and colleagues have termed psychological capital, or PsyCap. This PsyCap was conceptualized as going beyond human capital (see Luthans & Youssef, 2004), and for a positive psychological resource to be included, it must be based on theory and research, have a valid measure, be open to development (i.e., state-like rather than trait-like), and have performance impact (Luthans, 2002a; Luthans, Youssef & Avolio, 2007). The positive psychological constructs of efficacy, optimism, hope, and resilience were determined to best meet the inclusion criteria, and the resulting multidimensional construct of PsyCap was defined as "an individual's positive psychological state of development characterized by (a) having confidence (efficacy) to take on and put in the necessary effort to succeed at challenging tasks; (b) making a positive attribution (optimism) about succeeding now and in the future; (c) persevering toward goals, and when necessary, redirecting paths to goals (hope) in order to succeed; and (d) when beset by problems and adversity, sustaining and bouncing back and even beyond (resilience) to attain success" (Luthans, Youssef, & Avolio, 2007, p. 3).

PsyCap has been theoretically (Luthans, Youssef & Avolio, 2007) and empirically (Luthans, Avolio, Avey & Norman, 2007) supported as a second-order, core construct, meaning that PsyCap as a whole accounts for more variance in important work outcomes than each of its constituent positive psychological resources of efficacy, hope, optimism, and resiliency. A recent meta-analysis indicates that this PsyCap has a positive relationship with desirable employee attitudes, behaviors, and performance (Avey, Reichard, Luthans & Mhatre, 2011). Specifically, over the past few years, PsyCap has been shown to be developable in employees (Luthans, Avey, Avolio & Peterson, 2010; Luthans, Avey & Patera, 2008) and to cause performance (Luthans et al., 2010; Peterson, Luthans, Avolio, Walumbwa & Zhang, 2011). Further, PsyCap has been found to predict unique variance in important employee attitudes and behaviors over and above their demographics, core-self evaluations, personality traits, and person-organization and person-job fit (Avey, Luthans & Youssef, 2010). There is also a growing number of studies refining and expanding the positive impact of PsyCap on outcomes such as stress (Avey, Luthans & Jensen, 2009), well-being (Avey,

Luthans, Smith & Palmer, 2010), team effectiveness (Walumbwa, Luthans, Avey & Oke, 2011), and organizational change (Avey, Wernsing & Luthans, 2008). However, missing from this rapidly expanding research literature is the impact that PsyCap may have on problem-solving and innovation, and the role that PsyCap may have when integrated with OB Mod in positively impacting these complex areas of problem solving and innovation.

Positivity as an Antecedent, Cueing Mechanism

According to positive psychologist Barbara Fredrickson's (1998, 2001, 2009) widely recognized broaden-and-build theory, positivity and negativity affect people in different ways. Negativity leads people to respond in particular, narrow action tendencies such as the fight/flight response (Frijda, 1986). Positivity, on the other hand, broadens thought-action tendencies, which refer to both physical action as well as cognitive action (Fredrickson & Losada, 2005). Due to this positivity induced broadening of thought-action tendencies, an individual's physical, intellectual, social, and psychological resources are built up, and these new resources become available to the individual long after the initial positive experience occurs (Fredrickson, 1998). In other words, positivity allows a person to build up psychological resources, such as those found in PsyCap, that we propose can be drawn upon to help solve problems and exhibit innovation. Importantly, in addition, we propose that such positivity may facilitate employees' receptiveness to OB Mod reinforcers such as contingent performance feedback (discussed next).

When problems arise, most people react to the negativity of the situation, relying on narrow behavioral scripts and focusing on narrow details of the situation (e.g., see the classic work by Easterbrook, 1959). However, for those who regularly experience positivity and have built-up their psychological resources (i.e., PsyCap), Fredrickson's broaden-and-build theory would predict that they view problems from a broader perspective and are able to be more innovative and produce better and more solutions due to a heightened ability to integrate thoughts and ideas (Fredrickson, 1998; Isen, 1987; Isen & Daubman, 1984).

In addition to the overall impact of positivity, we propose that PsyCap and its constituent positive resources of efficacy, optimism, hope, and resilience are also likely to be related to innovation and the quality and quantity of problem solving in more specific ways. Underlying the core construct of PsyCap is a cognitive, agentic capacity representing "one's positive appraisal of circumstances and probability for success based on motivated effort and perseverance" (Luthans, Avolio, et al., 2007, p. 550). For example, this agentic capacity can be manifested in terms of a broader range of hope pathways (e.g., see Snyder, 2000), which can be particularly relevant for innovatively developing a wider range of higher quality solutions when faced with obstacles. It can also motivate the perseverance and ability to resiliently bounce back in reaction to setbacks (e.g., see Masten, 2001), which may be a necessary mindset for effective problem solving. A positive, optimistic outlook can facilitate this broadening effect on problem solving (e.g., see Seligman, 1998) and can heighten the desire for success and confidence that one has what it takes to develop the necessary range of action plans needed to solve a problem (Bandura, 1997). Thus, the following is hypothesized:

> Hypothesis 1a: PsyCap is positively related to problem solving performance.
> Hypothesis 1b: PsyCap is positively related to reported innovation.

Contingent Positive Feedback as a Reinforcing Mechanism

The antecedent, cueing impact of positivity in general, and the positive nature of PsyCap in particular, on problem-solving performance and reported innovation, can also be extrapolated to the positivity of the contingent performance feedback provided to the problem solver. However, we believe the time has come to go beyond just this antecedent positive cueing and even beyond the recognized reinforcing impact of contingent performance feedback as found in the OB Mod literature (Stajkovic & Luthans, 1997). Although the behavioral management literature recognizes there may be an optimal ratio of positive to negative in areas such as feedback to employees (e.g., Daniels recommends a 4:1 rule of positive reinforcement to criticism, 2000, p. 74), for this study we draw from the recently emerging research in positive psychology. More specifically, in work relationships, a positive-to-negative ratio of about 3:1 has been empirically found to be optimal, or a tipping point between flourishing and languishing in work relationships (Fredrickson, 2009, Chapter 7). In other words, employees' performance will likely dramatically differ, both qualitatively and quantitatively, not just based on how much positive feedback they receive, but possibly even more based on the ratio of positive to negative feedback they receive.

We test this differential notion by uniquely conceptualizing and operationalizing reinforcing feedback in terms of the relative positive-to-negative ratio, rather than just an absolute or linear amount of positive feedback. We propose, although positive contingent performance feedback is invaluable in and of itself (ala OB Mod), both as a positive antecedent, cueing mechanism, and as a reinforcer, a more positive than negative ratio of feedback can help problem solvers overcome the common human negativity bias (Baumeister, Bratslavsky, Finkenauer & Vohs, 2001). This more positive than negative ratio for feedback can reach an optimal positivity tipping point, leading to more effective problem-solving performance and reported innovation. Thus, the following is hypothesized:

Hypothesis 2a: A more positive than negative ratio of contingent performance feedback is positively related to problem-solving performance.

Hypothesis 2b: A more positive than negative ratio of contingent performance feedback is positively related to reported innovation.

A Mastery-Oriented Mindset as a Mediating Process

Mastery orientation refers to learning goals and behavioral patterns that are characterized by challenge seeking and persistence in the face of obstacles (Dweck, 1986; Dweck & Leggett, 1988; Mueller & Dweck, 1998). In addition to the direct contribution of PsyCap and a more positive than negative ratio of contingent performance feedback to problem-solving performance and reported innovation hypothesized above, we also propose an indirect relationship, mediated through a mastery-oriented mindset, for several reasons. First, cognitive states of positivity, such as those created through high PsyCap and a more positive than negative ratio of contingent performance feedback, can facilitate the building of psychological resources that allow employees to seek challenges and fulfill learning goals, i.e., a mastery oriented mindset, even when problems arise. Second, the underlying agentic cognitive component of PsyCap can yield favorable appraisals of the probability for success in unique situations. These positive appraisals in turn can provide the additional motivation necessary for the challenge-seeking characteristic of such a mastery orientation. Similarly, we propose that the informative content of feedback recognized in the OB Mod literature (see Stajkovic & Luthans, 1997) can be particularly relevant in building the motivation for mastery orientation. This assures the feedback recipient of having what it takes to be effective and successful.

Third, PsyCap's constituent capacities can individually and in concert contribute the necessary specific support for mastery orientation, such as confidence in one's abilities, optimistic future expectancies, hopeful thinking, and resilient perseverance. The social support dimension of more positive than negative ratio of contingent performance feedback can also mobilize similar cognitive, as well as affective and social, resources that are supportive of a mastery-oriented mindset. This social support communicates to the feedback recipients that others also have a vested interest in their success. Contrary to mastery orientation is what Dweck and colleagues refer to as "performance goals." Although sounding desirable, this is a helpless orientation characterized by a narrow focus on immediate expectations, avoiding challenges, and having low persistence in the face of adversity (Dweck, 1986; Dweck & Leggett, 1988; Mueller & Dweck, 1998). We propose that those with low PsyCap will likely have such a helpless orientation, because they would lack the confidence, willpower, waypower, perseverance, and positive expectancies necessary to seek challenges. For example, lack of optimism has been particularly associated with helplessness

(Seligman, 1998). Taken together, based on these three mechanisms, the following is hypothesized:

> Hypothesis 3a: PsyCap is positively related to mastery orientation.
> Hypothesis 3b: The more positive than negative ratio of contingent performance feedback is positively related to mastery orientation.

We also propose that those with mastery-oriented goals in turn will have higher problem-solving performance and reported innovation because these goals encourage them to seek challenges in order to master skills. This mastery process would likely motivate people to exhibit "out-of-the-box" thinking, curiosity, exploration, and experimentation leading to more effective problem-solving performance and reported innovation. On the other hand, Dweck's performance goals, despite the positive connotation of the term, are likely to negatively contribute to people's problem-solving performance and reported innovation, because such goals lead them to choose easy tasks and avoid failure. In other words, similar to positivity, mastery orientation may have a broadening effect, while performance orientation may have a narrowing effect. This is also in line with the existing support for the fundamental differences between the positive impact of "approach goals" and the negative impact of "avoidance goals" (Carver & Scheier, 1999; Elliot & Sheldon, 1997; Elliot, Sheldon & Church, 1997). Thus, the following is hypothesized:

> Hypothesis 4a: Mastery orientation is positively related to problem-solving performance.
> Hypothesis 4b: Mastery orientation is positively related to reported innovation.

Closing the Positivity Loop: The Upward Spiral of Positivity

In addition to the hypothesized positive relationship of PsyCap, more positive than negative ratio of contingent performance feedback, and mastery-oriented mindset with problem-solving performance and reported innovation, we propose these three factors can also increase future positivity (i.e., operationally defined here as PsyCap), triggering an upward spiral of flourishing and thriving (Cameron, Dutton & Quinn, 2003). Several processes can trigger this upward positivity spiral. First, as a developmental, state-like resource, PsyCap can be built and nurtured over time through increased confidence, hope, optimism, and resiliency (Luthans, Youssef, & Avolio, 2007). Specifically, overall PsyCap and its facets can be developed through intentional activities that leverage personal mastery, vicarious learning, social support, physiological and psychological arousal, goal setting, contingency planning, positive attributions, and effective coping and risk-management strategies (Luthans et al., 2010). These intentional activities can increase levels of positivity and well-being in general (Lyubomirsky, 2007), and we propose the resultant increased cognitive, agentic capacity can facilitate more positive appraisals of future circumstances and success expectancies. In other words, positivity can beget more positivity. This can be explained by recognized contagion (Barsade, 2002), spillover (Judge & Illies, 2004), and crossover effects (Bakker, Westman & Van Emmerik, 2009) and is also in line with the existing support for happiness as a process, rather than a destination (Diener & Oishi, 2005; Lyubomirsky, Sheldon, & Schkade, 2005).

Beyond self-evaluation, feedback can provide an external resource for both the additional cognitive informative content, as well as the social persuasion and support necessary for developing future positivity (PsyCap). Specifically, we propose the more positive than negative ratio of contingent performance feedback can move recipients to distinctively higher levels of positivity. Finally, mastery has been supported as a critical factor in developing efficacy (Bandura, 1997), an integral component of PsyCap. A mastery orientation would likely create the right medium for the development of efficacy in general, through challenge-seeking behavior and perseverance, leading to the development of efficacy, and PsyCap in general. Thus, the following is hypothesized.

> Hypothesis 5a: PsyCap is positively related to future PsyCap.
> Hypothesis 5b: More positive than negative ratio of contingent performance feedback is positively related to future PsyCap.
> Hypothesis 5c: Mastery orientation is positively related to future PsyCap.

METHOD

Procedure

The sample for this study consisted of a broad cross-section of 1,526 employees who agreed to participate in a large Midwestern university sponsored research project. The initial e-mail to all those who volunteered had them provide their consent on the IRB form and contained a link to the Time 1 online data collection. Upon following the link, participants were asked to read a short (one page) case study problem and provide solutions. When the participants were done providing solutions to this case problem, they were asked to complete a short survey assessing their demographics, psychological capital, and reported innovation.

Approximately 24 to 48 hours after completing the Time 1 survey, participants were e-mailed predetermined (according to various positive to negative ratios) but randomly assigned feedback regardless of how they performed on the case problem in Time 1. They were also given the link to the Time 2 survey, where they were asked to solve another one-page case study problem. Importantly, however, participants were asked to choose the level of difficulty of this second case. All were told that the first case was of medium difficulty, and they were now asked to choose another medium level case or an easier or more difficult one. However, the participants were all given the same case study at Time 2 regardless of their choice. PsyCap and innovation were also assessed at Time 2.

Sample Demographics

Participants were 57.3% female. The sample was 81.9% Caucasian/White, 2.6% African American, 2.0% Hispanic, 10.2% Asian, and 3.4% other. The mean age was 37.04 years ($SD=14.81$). As to industry, 10.7% worked in manufacturing, 52.0% in service, 15.4% worked in knowledge jobs, and 21.9% in other. The sample consisted of 65.8% full-time employees, 23.6% part-time employees, 4% seasonal workers, and 6.6% were currently unemployed. The mean job tenure was 10.35 years ($SD=10.74$). In total, the large sample was heterogeneous but representative of a broad range of jobs and career stages. Importantly, these demographics were controlled for in the analysis.

The Case Problems and Measures

The researchers plus two outside experts on the case method unanimously selected from a variety of alternatives a case study relevant to the modern scene that involved some personnel dynamics (i.e., interpersonal conflict) in the form of the transfer of a regional star performer from China to the home office in France. This served as the problem for participants to provide alternative solutions at Time 1. The second case study selected for Time 2 used the same selection group and met the same criteria. It involved Generation Y in the work force and contained the same underlying general theme of interpersonal conflict. Both these problem cases were adapted and paraphrased from a pool of case studies published in the *Harvard Business Review* (Erickson, Alsop, Nicholson, & Miller, 2009; Nohria, Tsang, Javidan, & Champy, 2009).

Positive Feedback

As indicated, in this study positive feedback was uniquely operationalized from a positive psychological perspective as the ratio of positive-to-negative comments received by each participant. This ratio was randomly varied for the study participants regardless of how they performed and was measured as the percentage of positive to total comments. Each participant received a total of eight comments, ranging from all positive (100%) to all negative (0%). Examples of positive feedback comments were "This solution will work" and "This is a good answer." An example of a negative feedback comment was "Your solution would not be effective."

MASTERY ORIENTATION

Mastery orientation was operationalized as the participant's Time 2 choice of a difficult, medium, or easy problem. Those who chose a difficult case were determined to have a higher mastery orientation.

PSYCHOLOGICAL CAPITAL

Psychological capital was measured at Time 1 and Time 2 using the PCQ-24 (see Luthans, Youssef, & Avolio, 2007 for the complete instrument and Luthans, Avolio, et al., 2007 for validation analysis). It utilized a 6-point Likert scale (1 = *strongly disagree* to 6 = *strongly agree*). A sample item was "At the present time, I am energetically pursuing my work goals." The Cronbach alpha for the measure of psychological capital in this study was .81 for both Time 1 and Time 2.

Performance Assessment

Performance was operationalized in three ways. There were two quality assessments of performance in solving the case studies and one quantity assessment of performance. Importantly, Time 1 performance measures on the case were used as control variables.

QUALITY ASSESSMENTS OF SOLUTIONS

Quality was assessed both objectively and subjectively. The objective measure of quality was operationalized as the average word count of all solutions produced by each participant. As word count is, of course, only a proxy for actual quality of solutions, we supplemented this objective measure with a subjective evaluation rating of quality. These evaluations rated the solutions for quality by three independent trained coders, blind to the study purpose and hypotheses. Coders assessed each solution using a 6 point scale (0–5). The coding criteria were developed by the researchers and the two case method experts. For example, better quality solutions addressed the salient interpersonal issues in the problem and provided a clear plan for how to implement the solution. Lower quality answers did not address the interpersonal issues of the case nor any type of plan of implementation. The interrater reliability among the three independent coders was .84 in Time 1 and .94 in Time 2. The average quality of all solutions produced by each participant was used as the quality of performance measure in the analysis.

QUANTITY ASSESSMENT OF SOLUTIONS

The quantity of solutions produced was assessed simply by counting how many solutions a participant submitted. There was ample room for participants to submit as many solutions as they desired. The maximum number of solutions submitted by any one participant in Time 1 was 5. In Time 2, the highest number of solutions given by any one participant was 9.

Reported Innovation

Reported innovation was measured using an 8-item scale adapted by Farmer, Tierney, and Kung-McIntyre (2003) from the source originality subscale of the Kirton Adaption-Innovation Inventory (KAI; Bobic, Davis, & Cunningham, 1999; Kirton, 1976). Participants were asked to indicate how much they agreed with statements such as "I would sooner create something than improve it" on a 6-point scale (strongly disagree to strongly agree). Cronbach's alpha for this innovation scale in this study was .71 in Time 1 and .75 in Time 2. Importantly, Time 1 innovation was used as a control variable.

RESULTS

Hierarchical regression analysis was used to test the study hypotheses. We conducted path analysis using a series of multiple regressions with all the variables preceding each variable included in the analyses that uses it as a dependent variable. We took this approach rather than employing SEM software to better accommodate the demographics, some of which are categorical variables, and to stay with recognized conventions for testing mediated models using regression (i.e., Baron & Kenny, 1986).

Figure 2 shows the significant relationships found in this study. After controlling for demographics and Time 1 performance and innovation, as shown PsyCap was positively related to mastery orientation, Time 2 innovation, and Time 2 PsyCap, but not to any of Time 2 problem-solving performance dimensions. Thus, Hypotheses 1b, 3a and 5a were supported, but Hypothesis 1a was not. The more positive than negative ratio of contingent performance feedback was positively related to average solution

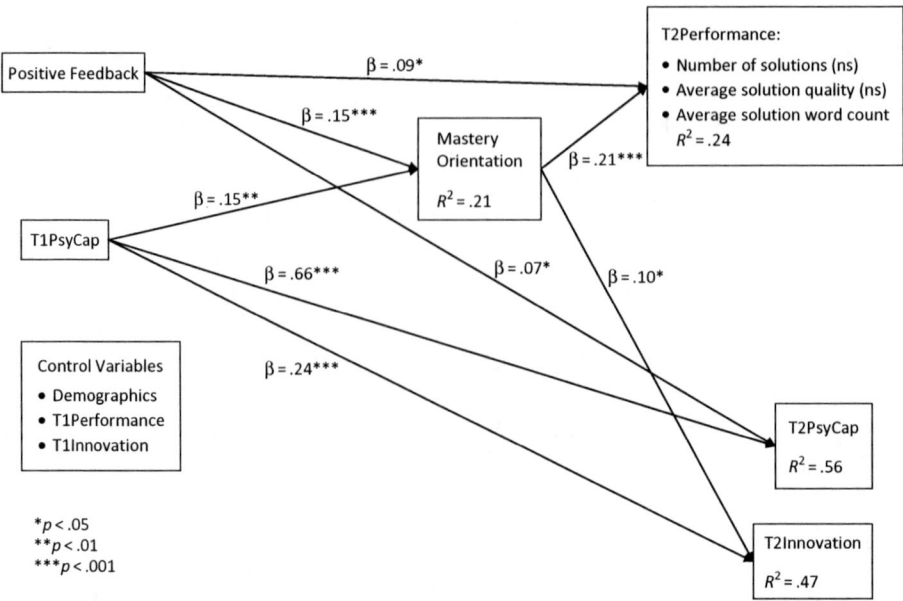

FIGURE 2 Significant results of study variable relationships.

word count, but not the other two dimensions of problem-solving performance. Thus, Hypothesis 2a was only partially supported. This same feedback was also related to Time 2 PsyCap and mastery orientation, but not to Time 2 Innovation. Thus, Hypotheses 3b and 5b were supported, but not Hypothesis 2b. Finally, mastery orientation was positively related to Time 2 innovation and average solution word count, but not to Time 2 PsyCap. Thus, Hypothesis 4b was supported, Hypothesis 4a was partially supported, and Hypothesis 5c was not supported. Following conventions for testing mediated models (Baron & Kenny, 1986), mastery orientation was supported as a partial mediator between Time 1 PsyCap and Time 2 Innovation, and between more positive than negative ratio feedback and average solution word count.

DISCUSSION

Drawing from both the established behavioral paradigm (i.e., OB Mod, Luthans & Kreitner, 1975, 1985; Stajkovic & Luthans, 1997) and the social-cognitive paradigm (i.e., positive organizational behavior or POB, Luthans, 2002a, 2002b; Luthans & Avolio, 2009; Luthans & Youssef, 2007; Wright, 2003), this quasi-experimental study found that positivity, operationalized as the now recognized multidimensional core construct of psychological capital (PsyCap; Luthans & Youssef, 2004; Luthans, Youssef, & Avolio, 2007) and feedback, operationalized as the more positive than negative ratio of contingent performance feedback comments, are generally related to important challenging and complex processes facing employees in today's organizations. Specifically, PsyCap was hypothesized as an antecedent cueing mechanism for more effective problem solving and potential innovative behavior, both directly and mediated through mastery-oriented goals and challenge-seeking behavior. Extrapolating from the OB Mod literature, the higher positive than negative ratios of feedback were hypothesized as potential reinforcers, and their impact was also tested both directly and mediated through mastery orientation. Overall, although there were some exceptions for the direct effects of both positive feedback and PsyCap, as seen in Figure 2 the results generally supported the theory driven hypotheses. The findings highlight the untapped potential of integrating established behavioral management with emerging positivity development approaches, specifically the potential impact on problem-solving performance and reported innovation.

Several theoretical contributions and practical implications can be drawn from these findings. First, in line with the emerging positivity research, PsyCap and positively weighted contingent performance feedback may have an additive effect in achieving a "tipping point" positive-to-negative ratio (recognized in behavioral management as 4:1, Daniels, 2000, and in positive psychology at about 3:1, Fredrickson & Losada, 2005). This offers managers and organizations with the evidence-based value of creating positive environments where the recognized role of more positive than negative feedback can be realistically applied and also leveraged further through the development and management of employees' PsyCap.

Second, using Fredrickson's (1998, 2001, 2009) broaden-and-build theory as a point of departure, the results of this study suggest the broadened thought-action repertoires and expanded inventory of psychological resources due to positivity can be particularly relevant for problem-solving performance and potentially enhanced innovation. This confirms the commonsense, conventional wisdom that employees are more creative when in a positive environment and mindset. Indeed, widely recognized positive culture companies such as Southwest Airlines and the software development firm SAS have successfully capitalized on such an environment for many years.

Third, the findings of this study provide a newly tested mediating mechanism for positivity, namely mastery orientation. Agentic, mastery-oriented learning goals and challenge-seeking behavior would seem to be critical for effective problem solving and innovation. Psychological capital and positive ratio feedback represent a new approach for building such mastery, which in turn may enhance the creative, innovative dimensions of performance. This finding can help managers design more focused approaches for developing creativity in their employees. In addition to developing employees' psychological capital and providing them with higher positive-to-negative ratios of feedback, the results of this study also point to the importance of helping them develop a mastery orientation and mindset.

Fourth, this study presents preliminary evidence for an upward spiral (contagion) of positivity. Specifically, Time 1 PsyCap was positively correlated to and accounted for unique variance in Time 2 PsyCap. Relatedly, this study also sheds light on the PsyCap development process. Even after accounting for demographics and Time 1 performance and innovation, both Time 1 PsyCap and positively dominant feedback accounted for unique variance in Time 2 PsyCap. This finding highlights the integral role that positive feedback may play in PsyCap development. For example, positive feedback can provide both the social persuasion necessary for efficacy building (Bandura, 1997) and the social support assets that have been found to be so critical in developing resilience (Masten, 2001).

Among the strengths of this study's design is the unique contribution of drawing from two paradigms (often pitted against one another over the years) to derive and test a new conceptual model that relates positive contingent feedback, psychological capital, and mastery orientation with a positive impact on problem-solving performance and innovation. The large, heterogeneous sample also provides for greater generalizability than smaller, more homogenous samples. The quasi-experimental design, random assignment and time separation in collecting independent and dependent variables helps minimize common method bias issues in the relationship between predictor and outcome variables (Podsakoff, MacKenzie, Lee, & Podsakoff, 2003) and allows for at least cautious causal inferences. Controlling for demographics and Time 1 performance and reported innovation also gives more credibility to the contribution of the study variables.

Regarding limitations, conceptually, there is an ongoing debate regarding the position of PsyCap on the trait-state continuum (see Luthans & Youssef, 2007 for an extensive treatment of this issue). Despite the strong relationship between Time 1 and Time 2 PsyCap, other variables accounted for unique variance, supporting the emerging experimental support for the state-like nature and developmental potential of PsyCap (Luthans, Avey, & Patera, 2008; Luthans et al., 2010). One particularly unique finding was that despite the extensive support for mastery as a recognized mechanism for developing the efficacy constituent of PsyCap, in this study mastery did not predict Time 2 PsyCap. A possible explanation may be the relatively short length of the study. Replications of this study should leverage longitudinal designs or growth models, where participants can be given adequate time to develop mastery before PsyCap is reassessed. Despite time separation, the relationship between PsyCap and innovation may be an artifact of same source bias.

In conclusion, the results suggest that positivity in general and psychological capital in particular may play an important role in learning goal or mastery orientation and innovation, and potentially, problem solving. These organizational behavior outcomes are especially impactful in these economic times, when layoffs and crises disrupt organizations and make interpersonal conflicts an everyday challenge, and problem-solving effectiveness and innovation can greatly contribute to competitive advantage. While the established behavioral approaches such as OB Mod have clearly been shown to increase performance, combining positively weighted feedback with other positive constructs such as PsyCap may leverage OB Mod's effect on performance to even higher levels and potentially contribute to complex processes such as problem solving and innovation. Positivity allows employees to transcend negative experiences in the workplace (or elsewhere), making the tried-and-true behavioral techniques even more effective.

REFERENCES

Avey, J. B., Luthans, F., & Jensen, S. (2009). Psychological capital: A positive resource for combating stress and turnover. *Human Resource Management, 48*, 677–693.

Avey, J. B., Luthans, F., Smith, R., & Palmer, N. (2010). Impact of positive psychological capital on employee well-being over time. *Journal of Occupational Health Psychology, 12*, 17–28.

Avey, J. B., Luthans, F., & Youssef, C. M. (2010). The additive value of positive psychological capital in predicting work attitudes and behaviors. *Journal of Management, 36*, 430–452.

Avey, J. B., Reichard, R., Luthans, F., & Mhatre, K. (2011). Meta-analysis of the impact of positive psychological capital on employee attitudes, behaviors and performance. *Human Resource Development Quarterly, 22*, 127–152.

Avey, J. B., Wernsing, T. S., & Luthans, F. (2008). Can positive employees help positive organization change? *The Journal of Applied Behavioral Science, 44*, 48–70.

Bakker, A. B., Westman, M., & Van Emmerik, I. J. H. (2009) Advances in crossover theory. *Journal of Managerial Psychology, 12*, 206–219.

Bandura, A. (1969). *Principles of behavior modification*. New York, NY: Holt, Rinehart, & Winston.

Bandura, A. (1997). *Self-efficacy*. New York, NY: Freeman.

Baron, R. M., & Kenny, D. A. (1986). The moderator-mediator variable distinction in social psychological research. *Journal of Personality & Social Psychology, 51*, 1173–1182.

Barsade, S. G. (2002). The ripple effect: Emotional contagion and its influence on group behavior. *Administrative Science Quarterly, 47*, 644–675.

Baumeister, R. F., Bratslavsky, E., Finkenauer, C., & Vohs, K. D. (2001). Bad is stronger than good. *Review of General Psychology, 5*, 323–370.

Bobic, M., Davis, E., & Cunningham, R. (1999). The Kirton adaptation-innovation inventory. *Review of Public Personnel Administration, 19*, 18–31.

Cameron, K. S., Dutton, J., & Quinn, R. (Eds.). (2003). *Positive organizational scholarship*. San Francisco, CA: Berrett-Koehler.

Carver, C. S., & Scheier, M. F. (1999). Themes and issues in the self-regulation of behavior. In R. S. Wyer, Jr, (Ed.), *Perspectives on behavioral self-regulation: Advances in social cognition* (Vol. 12; 1–105). Mahwah, NJ: Erlbaum.

Daniels, A. R. (2000). *Bringing out the best in people: The astonishing power of positive reinforcement* (2nd ed.). New York, NY: McGraw-Hill.

Diener, E., & Oishi, S. (2005). The nonobvious social psychology of happiness. *Psychological Inquiry, 16*, 162–167.

Dweck, C. (1986). Motivational processes affecting learning. *American Psychologist, 41*, 1040–1048.

Dweck, C. & Leggett, E. (1988). A social-cognitive approach to motivation and personality. *Psychological Review, 95*(2), 256–273.

Easterbrook, J. A. (1959). The effect of emotion on cue utilization and the organization of behavior. *Psychological Review, 66*, 83–201.

Elliot, A.J., & Sheldon, K.M. (1997). Avoidance achievement motivation: A personal goals analysis. *Journal of Personality and Social Psychology, 73*, 171–185.

Elliot, A. J., Sheldon, K. M., & Church, M. A. (1997). Avoidance personal goals and subjective well-being. *Personality and Social Psychology Bulletin, 23*, 915–927.

Erickson, T., Alsop, R., Nicholson, P., & Miller, J. (2009). Gen Y in the workforce. *Harvard Business Review, 87*(2), 43–49.

Farmer, S. M., Tierney, P., & Kung-McIntypre, K. (2003). Employee creativity in Taiwan: An application of role identity theory. *Academy of Management Journal, 45*, 1137–1148.

Fredrickson, B. L. (1998). What good are positive emotions? *Review of General Psychology, 2*, 300–319.

Fredrickson, B. L. (2001). The role of positive emotions in positive psychology: The broaden-and-build theory of positive emotions. *American Psychologist, 56*, 218–226.

Fredrickson, B. L. (2009). *Positivity*. New York, NY: Crown Publishers.

Fredrickson, B. L., & Losada, M. F. (2005). Positive affect and the complex dynamics of human flourishing. *American Psychologist, 60*, 678–686.

Frijda, N. J. (1986). *The emotions*. Cambridge, England: Cambridge University Press.

Isen, A. M. (1987). Positive affect facilitates creative problem solving. *Journal of Personality and Social Psychology, 52*, 1122–1131.

Isen, A. M., & Daubman, K. A. (1984). The influence of affect on categorization. *Journal of Personality and Social Psychology, 47*, 1206–1217.

Judge, T. A., & Illies, R. (2004). Affect and job satisfaction. *Journal of Applied Psychology, 89*, 661–673.

Kirton, M. (1976). Adaptors and Innovators: A description and a measure. *Journal of Applied Psychology, 61*, 266–629.

Luthans, F. (1973). *Organizational behavior*. New York, NY: McGraw-Hill.

Luthans, F. (2002a). The need for and meaning of positive organizational behavior. *Journal of Organizational Behavior, 23*, 695–706.

Luthans, F. (2002b). Positive organizational behavior: Developing and managing psychological strengths. *Academy of Management Executive, 16*, 57–72.

Luthans, F., Avey, J. B., Avolio, B. J., & Peterson, S. J. (2010). The development and resulting performance impact of positive psychological capital. *Human Resource Development Quarterly, 21*, 41–67.

Luthans, F., Avey, J. B., & Patera, J. L. (2008). Experimental analysis of a web-based intervention to develop positive psychological capital. *Academy of Management Learning and Education, 7*, 209–221.

Luthans, F., & Avolio, B. J. (2009). The "point" of positive organizational behavior. *Journal of Organizational Behavior, 30*, 291–307.

Luthans, F., Avolio, B. J., Avey, J. B., & Norman, S. M. (2007). Positive psychological capital: Measurement and relationship with performance and satisfaction. *Personnel Psychology, 60*, 541–572.

Luthans, F., Fox, M., & Davis, T. (1991). Improving the delivery of quality service: Behavioral management techniques. *Leadership and Organizational Development Journal, 12*(2), 3–6.

Luthans, F., & Kreitner, R. (1975). *Organizational behavior modification*. Glenview, IL: Scott Foresman.

Luthans, F., & Kreitner, R. (1985). *Organizational behavior modification and beyond*. Glenview, IL: Scott Foresman.

Luthans, F., Paul, R., & Baker, D. (1981). An experimental analysis of the impact of contingent reinforcement on salespersons' performance behavior. *Journal of Applied Psychology, 66*, 314–323.

Luthans, F., Rhee, S., Luthans, B. C., & Avey, J. (2008). Impact of behavioral performance management in a Korean application. *Leadership and Organization Development Journal, 29*, 427–443.

Luthans, F., & Youssef, C. M. (2004). Human, social, and now positive psychological capital management. *Organizational Dynamics, 33*, 143–160.

Luthans, F., & Youssef, C. M. (2007). Emerging positive organizational behavior. *Journal of Management, 33*, 321–349.

Luthans, F., Youssef, C. M., & Avolio, B. J. (2007). *Psychological capital: Developing the human competitive edge*. Oxford, England: Oxford University Press.

Lyubomirsky, S. (2007). *The how of happiness: A new approach to getting the life you want*. New York, NY: Penguin.

Lyubomirsky, S., Sheldon, K. M., & Schkade, D. (2005). Pursuing happiness: The architecture of sustainable change. *Review of General Psychology, 9*, 111–131.

Masten, A. S. (2001). Ordinary magic: Resilience process in development. *American Psychologist, 56*, 227–239.

Mueller, C., & Dweck, C. (1998). Praise for intelligence can undermine children's motivation and performance. *Journal of Personality and Social Psychology, 75*(1), 33–52.

Nohria, M., Tsang, K., Javidan, M., & Champy, J. (2009). From regional star to global leader. *Harvard Business Review, 87*(1), 33–39.

Pavlov, I. (1927). *Conditioned reflexes: An investigation of the physiological activity of the cerebral cortex*. Oxford, England: Oxford University Press.

Peterson, S. J., & Luthans, F. (2006). The impact of financial and non-financial incentives on business-unit outcomes over time. *Journal of Applied Psychology, 91*, 156–165.

Peterson, S. J., Luthans, F., Avolio, B. J., Walumbwa, F. O., & Zhang, Z. (2011). Psychological capital and employee performance: A latent growth modeling approach. *Personnel Psychology, 64*, 427–450.

Podsakoff, R. M., MacKenzie, S. C., Lee, J., & Podsakoff, N. P. (2003). Common method biases in behavioral research: A critical review of the literature and recommended remedies. *Journal of Applied Psychology, 88,* 879–903.

Seligman, M. E. P. (1998). *Learned optimism.* New York, NY: Pocket Books.

Seligman, M. E. P., & Csikszentmihalyi, M. (2000). Positive psychology. *American Psychologist, 55,* 5–14.

Skinner, B. (1938). *The behavior of organisms.* New York, NY: Appleton-Century-Crofts.

Snyder, C. R. (2000). *Handbook of hope.* San Diego, CA: Academic Press.

Snyder, C. R., & Lopez, S. (Eds.). (2002). *Handbook of positive psychology.* Oxford, England: Oxford University Press.

Stajkovic, A., & Luthans, F. (1997). A meta-analysis of the effects of organizational behavior modification on task performance, 1975–95. *Academy of Management Journal, 40,* 1122–1149.

Stajkovic, A., & Luthans, F. (2001). Differential effects of incentive motivators on work performance. *Academy of Management Journal, 44,* 580–590.

Stajkovic, A., & Luthans, F. (2003). Behavioral management and task performance in organizations: Conceptual background, meta-analysis, and test of alternative models. *Personnel Psychology, 56,* 155–194.

Thorndike, E. (1913). *Educational psychology: The psychology of learning* (Vol. 2). New York, NY: Columbia University Teachers College.

Walumbwa, F. O., Luthans, F., Avey, J. B., & Oke, A. (2011). Authentically leading groups: The mediating role of collective psychological capital and trust. *Journal of Organizational Behavior, 32,* 4–24.

Wright, T. A. (2003). Positive organizational behavior. *Journal of Organizational Behavior, 24,* 437–442.

Employee Engagement and Organizational Behavior Management

TIMOTHY D. LUDWIG and CHRISTOPHER B. FRAZIER
Appalachian State University, Boone, North Carolina, USA

Engagement is a "buzz" word that has gained popularity in Industrial/Organizational Psychology. Based on a "Positive Psychology" approach, engagement is perceived as a valuable state for employees, because surveys on the construct have found it correlates with some organizational tactics (e.g., human resource policies, procedural justice) and positive outcomes (e.g., growth, lower costs, lower absenteeism). Reviews of the engagement literature suggest engagement is not clearly defined, which is common with some popular cognitive/emotional constructs. Positive Psychology is nothing new to behavior analysis (Luthans, Youssef, & Rawski, 2011), which has many applications through the field of Organizational Behavior Management to create an "engaged" workforce and culture.

Employee engagement is a young and indistinct construct within organizational research yet to be clearly defined. Nonetheless, it has become the latest "buzz" word in management, sparking opportunistic interest in the academic field. However, from a behavior analytic perspective, employees' "vigor" and "energy" may be simply a matter of managing contingencies through the behavioral systems that include operational and managerial processes.

Employee engagement is not a well-defined construct, as many authors define it differently. According to the *Gallup Employee Engagement Survey*

Analysis Tool (*ESAT*; Corporate Leadership Council, 2009) survey, engagement can be broken into rational and emotional engagement. Rational engagement is defined as "the extent to which employees believe that managers, teams, or organizations have their self interest in mind (financial, developmental, or professional)," while emotional engagement is defined as "the extent to which employees value, enjoy, and believe in their jobs, managers, teams or organizations" (p. 4). Towers Perrin (2003) defines engagement as "employees' willingness and ability to contribute to company success . . . the extent to which employees put discretionary effort into their work" (p. 1). Macey and Schneider (2008) add that engagement contains organizational citizenship behaviors (OCB).

Moreover, engagement has been described as made up of different psychological states (or at least is correlated with states) such as involvement, attachment, mood (Macey & Schneider, 2008), job satisfaction, and organizational commitment (Saks, 2006; Wefald, & Downey, 2008). Positive Affectivity has also been highly correlated with engagement (Macey & Schneider, 2008). Of course, the causal directionality and "third variable" problem is pervasive in this research, because it is unclear if these psychological states lead to engagement, if engagement leads to these states, or if these states all covary with another variable altogether (e.g., company success).

Variables that lead to engagement are numerous. A highly correlated variable in Saks' (2006) review, as well as the large-scale study produced by Towers Perrin (2003), was job characteristics (cf., Hackman & Oldham, 1976). These include challenging work, autonomy over decisions, and career advancement opportunities. Saks (2006) argued employees must be given adequate resources to get their job done well. Auxiliary policies and facilities such as a day care center, gym, and cafeteria help employees balance their lives more efficiently with more flexibility, supposedly leading to engagement (Foursight Consulting, 2005; McLeish, 2008; Pitt-Catsouphes & Matz-Costa, 2008; Schaufeli & Bakker, 2004).

Management behavior moderates the relationship between engagement and organizational outcomes (e.g., sales) and therefore can influence employee behavior (Smith, Huelsman, Bergman, & Ludwig, 2010). Blessing White, Inc. (2008) state that managers must be engaged for their subordinates to be engaged. Additionally, survey data suggest that management must be customer focused, communicate effectively, and have the employees' well-being as a high priority to produce engaged employees (Towers Perrin, 2003) because they have built "trust" (Chughtai & Buckley, 2008). Organizational variables that may be related to engagement include human resources, policies, values, culture, technology, etc. (Towers Perrin, 2003) that promote a perception of procedural justice (i.e., how fair employees perceive the processes around outcomes; Saks, 2006).

Correlational research suggests the outcomes of engagement are indeed impressive, as they speak directly to business results (Hyten, 2009).

Employee engagement been shown to be positively correlated to higher revenue growth, a lower cost of goods sold, and negatively correlated with intentions to quit/turnover (Saks, 2006; Towers Perrin, 2003). Organizations in the top quartile of employee engagement accrued 1% to 4% more in organizational profits annually (Harter, Schmidt & Hayes, 2002). However, the causality or directionality of such statements remain suspect. It is unclear whether engagement creates the successful organizations or if successful organizations make employees more engaged or if both are a result of another variable such as managerial behavior (Smith et al., 2010).

Saks (2008) states, "The engagement concept . . . needs to be role specific rather than a cocktail of related constructs," (pp. 42–43) and thereby disagrees with defining engagement as merely job satisfaction, organizational commitment, or an outcome of management caring (Saks, 2009). Saks (2008) suggests that "behavioral engagement" should be the research construct of interest because it is observable and is most directly related to human performance and the bottom line. We agree with Saks' (2008, 2009) assessment as well as A. C. Daniels (2009), who states that engagement is simply "a non-specific non-scientific term used to describe the amount of positive reinforcement available in a workplace for value-added behavior" (p. 7).

ORGANIZATIONAL BEHAVIOR MANAGEMENT: AN ALTERNATIVE VIEW OF ENGAGEMENT

A. C. Daniels (2009) argues a key variable that drives all organizational outcomes is human behavior: "If management practices, systems, and processes are not designed on the basis of known facts about behavior, no organization can expect to create a workplace where all employees consistently give their best" (p. 7). Indeed, the variables associated with engagement above are not uncommon to the science of behavior analysis applied to organizations called Organizational Behavior Management (OBM), which works on improving behavior without being concerned with or attempting to change psychological traits, states, or other covert phenomena.

Reinforcement

A. C. Daniels (2009) suggests positive reinforcement is the most efficient way to make behavior effective and create the kind of organizational cultural behaviors that are credited to engagement. According to Daniels, positive reinforcement has to be personal, immediate, contingent on behavior, and frequent. Geller (2003) recommends noncontingent rewards over positive reinforcement, because it can be used to recognize individuals and groups with financial or social outcomes. When delivered effectively by management, such rewards can have a profound effect on a positive work environment. Geller (2003) suggests rewards create pleasant personal states as a consequence of receiving them. Skinner (1974) noted that positive results stemming from behavior can create a positive psychological state such as happiness. Gravina (2011) too suggests that responses to common organizational survey measurements, such as job satisfaction, organizational commitment, or even engagement, are classically conditioned responses. Also, Mawhinney (2011), in this issue, argues convincingly that "cumulative effects of reinforcers (punishers) contingent on performances will account for variations in performance-related satisfaction." Perhaps engagement is the label for the classically conditioned response to the copious amount of social and other reinforcement associated with value-added behavior.

Adequate Resources

Deming (1986) famously said that it is management's job to remove the barriers to employees' success. OBM takes a similar view whereby availability of resources serves as an antecedent to promote behaviors and to ensure that behaviors are maintained with the proper reinforcers. Take, for example, a story told by Ludwig (2011) where a manager complained that workers were not doing housekeeping in an industrial plant. After an assessment of antecedents and consequences, it was found that workers did not have the right tools conveniently located proximal to their housekeeping behaviors. Providing those resources (step ladders and work sinks) increased the behavior regardless of any increase in an "engagement" score.

Management Behaviors

Many management actions that create "engaged" employees can be explained from an OBM perspective and applied through intervention. OBM research is full of empirically tested communication tools: task clarification (Crowell, Anderson, Able, & Sergio, 1988; Rice, Austin, & Gravina, 2009; Slowiak, Madden, & Mathews, 2005), goal setting (Ludwig & Geller, 1997; Tittelbach, DeAngelis, Sturmey, & Alvero, 2007), checklists (Eikenhout, & Austin, 2005; Rodriguez et al., 2005), posted policies (Squires et al., 2007), and explicit rules (Johnson, Houmanfar, & Smith, 2010).

A related issue to management communication is management consistency. OBM research emphasizes the use of Behavioral Systems Analysis, including process maps of the managerial processes (Diener, McGee, & Miguel, 2009) to reveal places where work procedures, tasks, and reinforcers are ambiguous. When these ambiguities are exposed and corrected, behaviors are better specified and reinforced, leading perhaps to the conditions attributed to "engagement."

A final management behavior that may be related to the conditions of engagement is performance feedback (Crowell et al., 1988; Rice et al., 2009; Squires et al., 2007; Tittelbach et al., 2007). A. C. Daniels and

J. E. Daniels (2004) explain that ambiguous verbal feedback can be a punisher and reduce behavior. Conversely, unambiguous feedback that is timely, objective, based on employee behavior, and linked to business results, goals, or valued consequences, can have a strong impact on behavior, especially if that behavior is self-generated.

Autonomy

Another aspect of engagement, also popular among noted social psychologists (Allport, 1937; Deci & Ryan, 1985) is the concept of autonomy. This aspect of engagement is argued to be related to a "positive" culture (Saks, 2006; Towers Perrin, 2003). Since cultural variables are primarily measured with survey research, there are very few behavioral examples of this relationship. However, A. C. Daniels (2000) and others (Geller, 2002) have pointed to what may be called "Discretionary Behavior," where employees go beyond what is discriminated by the reinforcers and engage in other behaviors that are desirable to the organization or community (OCB, in I/O Psychology terminology; Macey & Scheider, 2008). OBM research has shown that when given the opportunity to set their own goals (i.e., implicit rules), employees generalize desirable behaviors beyond the original targeted behaviors specified in the goals (Ludwig, 2001; Ludwig & Geller, 1997). Ludwig and Geller (1997, 2001) call this phenomena "response generalization" and also suggest that there is a causal relationship between participatory intervention tactics and response generalization (Ludwig, 2001). Thus, when managers change the job design to allow for more autonomous behaviors, they may indeed find employees engaging in desirable behaviors beyond the original "targeted" suggestions (A. C. Daniels, 2009; Ludwig, 2001).

Experimental Causality

It is easy for organizations to gather data from their employees by giving them surveys that may tell them valuable information (Blessing White, Inc., 2008). However, it is much more difficult for those organizations to utilize that information for effective behavior change. All of the engagement studies reviewed above were based on correlational explorations between survey data, psychological questionnaires, and organizational data. While these exploratory studies may direct us toward high-impact interventions whose impact maintains over time and may generalize to other behaviors, discretionary and otherwise, they are severely limited in the practical, causal advice they can offer the practitioner. Indeed when investigating the Gallup company's survey approach to engagement, which they sell for tens of thousands of dollars, we found that after the survey results are completed they only suggest that focus groups be convened to brainstorm how engagement can be improved.

In contrast, behavior change in OBM studies is demonstrated with robust repeated measures (within) experimental designs (e.g., ABA reversal, multiple baselines) gaining inferences of substantial causal relationships (Cook & Cambell, 1979; Kazdin, 1982). Thus, the OBM community is in a far better position to advise practitioners on specific methods to garner broad performance improvement in a workforce.

We believe that research should continue to be conducted linking the correlational findings around engagement to OBM practices and behavioral change. When OBM can fill the gap left by Industrial/Organizational Psychology research through expanded terminology and scope (Geller, 2003; Weigland & Geller, 2004), then it may indeed find itself back in the mainstream of organizational literature and practice.

REFERENCES

Allport, G. W. (1937). The functional autonomy of motives. *American Journal of Psychology, 50*, 141–156.

Blessing White, Inc. (2008). The state of employee engagement. *North American Overview*. Retrieved from http://www.blessingwhite.com/EEE__report.asp

Chughtai, A. A., & Buckley, F. (2008). Work engagement and its relationship with state and trait trust: A conceptual analysis. *Journal of Behavioral and Applied Management, 10*, 47–71.

Cook, T. D., & Campbell, D. T. (1979). *Quasi-experimentation: Design and analysis for field settings*. Chicago, IL:. Rand McNally.

Corporate Leadership Council. (2009, October). *Employee engagement survey and analysis tool (ESAT)*. Unpublished.

Crowell, C. R., Anderson, D. C., Able, D. M., & Sergio, J. P. (1988). Task clarification, performance feedback, and social praise: Procedures for improving customer service of bank tellers. *Journal of Applied Behavior Analysis, 21*, 65–71.

Daniels, A. C. (2000). *Bringing out the best in people: How to apply the astonishing power of positive reinforcement* (2nd ed.). New York, NY: McGraw-Hill.

Daniels, A. C. (2009). *Oops! 13 management practices that waste time and money (and what to do instead)*. Atlanta, GA: Performance Management.

Daniels, A. C., & Daniels, J. E. (2004). *Performance management: Changing behavior that drives organizational effectiveness*. Atlanta, GA: Performance Management.

Deci, E. L., & Ryan, R.M. (1985). *Intrinsic motivation and self determination in human behavior*. New York, NY: Plenum.

Deming, W. E. (1986). *Out of the crisis*. Cambridge, MA: MIT Press.

Diener, L. H., McGee, H. M., & Miguel, C. F. (2009). An integrated approach for conducting a behavioral systems analysis. *Journal of Organizational Behavior Management, 29*, 108–135.

Eikenhout, N., & Austin, J. (2005). Using goals, feedback, reinforcement, and a performance matrix to improve customer service in a large department store. *Journal of Organizational Behavior Management, 24*(3), 27–62. doi:10.1300/J075v24n0302

Foursight Consulting. (2005). Focus on innovation. *Foursight Consulting Newsletter, 2*(10), 1–3.

Geller, E. S. (2002). *The participation factor: How to increase involvement in occupational safety*. Des Plaines, IL: American Society of Safety Engineers.

Geller, E. S. (2003). Should Organizational Behavior Management expand its content? *Journal of Organizational Behavior Management, 22*(2), 13–30.

Gravina, N. (2011, March). *Are you there OBM? It's me, business*. Presented at the Organizational Behavior Management Network Conference, Tampa, FL.

Hackman J. R., & Oldham, G. R. (1976). Motivation through design of work. *Organizational behaviour and human performance, 16*, 250–279.

Harter, J. K., Schmidt, F. L., & Hayes, T. L. (2002). Business-unit level relationship between employee satisfaction, employee engagement, and business outcomes: A meta-analysis. *Journal of Applied Psychology, 87*, 268–279.

Hyten, C. (2009) Strengthening the focus on business results: The need for systems approaches in Organizational Behavior Management. *Journal of Organizational Behavior Management, 29*(2), 87–107.

Johnson, R. A., Houmanfar R., & Smith, G. S. (2010). The effect of implicit and explicit rules on customer greeting and productivity in a retail organization. *Journal of Organizational Behavior Management, 30*, 38–48. doi:10.1080/01608060903529731

Kazdin, A. E. (1982). *Single-case research designs*. New York, NY: Oxford University Press.

Ludwig, T. D. (2001). On the necessity of structure in an arbitrary world: Using concurrent schedules of reinforcement to describe response generalization. *Journal of Organizational Behavior Management, 21*(4), 13–37.

Ludwig, T. D. (2011). What you learn from falling on your butt. *Industrial Safety & Health News, 45*(5), 38–39.

Ludwig, T. D., & Geller, E. S. (1997). Assigned versus participative goal setting and response generalization: Managing injury control among professional pizza drivers. *Journal of Applied Psychology, 82*, 253–261.

Luthans, F., Youssef, C. M., & Rawski, S. L. (2011). A tale of two paradigms: The impact of psychological capital and reinforcing feedback on problem solving and innovation. *Journal of Organizational Behavior Management, 31*, 333–350.

Macey, W. H., & Schneider, B. (2008). The meaning of employee engagement. *Industrial and Organizational Psychology, 1*, 3–30.

Mawhinney, T. C. (2011). Job satisfaction: I/O Psychology and Organizational Behavior Management perspectives. *Journal of Organizational Behavior Management, 31*, 288–315.

McLeish, J., (2008). Google's #1 again! *Employee Engagement Network*. Retrieved from http://employeeengagement.ning.com/profiles/blogs/1986438:BlogPost:217

Pitt-Catsouphes, M., & Matz-Costa, C. (2008). The multi-generational workforce: Workplace flexibility and engagement. *Community, Work, & Family, 11*(2), 215–229.

Rice, A., Austin J., & Gravina, N. (2009). Increasing customer service behaviors using manager-delivered task clarification and social praise. *Journal of Applied Behavior Analysis, 42,* 665–669.

Rodriguez, M., Wilder, D., Therrien, K., Wine, B., Miranti, R., Daratany, K., . . . Rodriguez, M. (2005). Use of the performance diagnostic checklist to select an intervention designed to increase the offering of promotional stamps at two sites of a restaurant franchise. *Journal of Organizational Behavior Management, 25,* 17–35. doi:10.1300/J075v25n03-02

Saks, A. M. (2006). Antecedents and consequences of employee engagement. *Journal of Managerial Psychology, 21,* 600–619.

Saks, A. M. (2008). The meaning and bleeding of employee engagement: How muddy is the water? *Industrial and Organizational Psychology, 1,* 40–43.

Saks, A. M. (2009). Engagement: The academic perspective. *Canadian HR Reporter, 22*(2), 31.

Schaufeli, W. B., & Bakker, A. B. (2004). Job demands, job resources, and their relationship with burnout and engagement: A multi-sample study. *Journal of Organizational Behavior, 25,* 293–315.

Skinner, B. F. (1974). *About behaviorism.* New York, NY: Random House.

Slowiak, J. M., Madden, G. J., & Mathews, R. (2005). The effects of a combined task clarification, goal setting, feedback, and performance contingent consequence intervention package on telephone customer service in a medical clinic environment. *Journal of Organizational Behavior Management, 25*(4), 15–35.

Smith, A., Huelsman, T. J., Bergman, J., & Ludwig, T. D. (2010, April). Adaptability: Does manager's competency matter after culture is controlled? Paper presented at the Society for Industrial and Organizational Psychology, Atlanta, GA.

Squires, J., Wilder, D., Fixsen, A., Hess, E., Rost, K., Curran, R., & Zonneveld, K. (2007). The effects of task clarification, visual prompts, and graphic feedback on customer greeting and up-selling in a restaurant. *Journal of Organizational Behavior Management, 27*(3), 1–13. doi:10.1300/J075v27n03_01

Tittelbach, D., DeAngelis, M., Sturmey, P., & Alvero, A. M. (2007). The effects of task clarification, feedback, and goal setting on student advisors' office behaviors and customer service. *Journal of Organizational Behavior Management, 27*(3), 27–40.

Towers Perrin. (2003). Working today: Understanding what drives employee engagement. *Towers Perrin Talent Report.* Retrieved from http://www.towersperrin.com/tp/getwebcachedoc?webc=hrs/usa/2003/200309/talent_2003.pdf

Wefald, A. J., & Downey, R. G. (2008). Job engagement in organizations: Fad, fashion or folderol? *Journal of Organizational Behavior, 30,* 141–145.

Wiegand, D. M., & Geller, E. S. (2004). Connecting positive psychology and organizational behavior management: Achievement motivation and the power of positive reinforcement. *Journal of Organizational Behavior Management, 24*(1/2), 3–25.

Index

Abernathy, W.B. 87
absenteeism 79, 88
Aguinis, H. 62–5, 84–5
Albrecht, K.; and Zemke, R. 104
Alvero, A.; Bucklin, B.R. and Austin, J.T. 66
antecendents 83
appraisals *see* performance appraisals
Association for Behavior Analysis (ABA) 88
Atieh, J.M.; and Brief, A.P. 7
Austin, J.T.: Alvero, A. and Bucklin, B.R. 66; and Villanova, P. 64, 112
Avolio, B.J.; Luthans, F. and Youssef, C.M. 119

Baer, D.M.; and Schwartz, I.S. 84–5, 91
bank balance sheet 56
Baum, W.M. 83–4
Bechtel Group 88
Beehr, T.A.: *et al* 79; and Johnson, C.M. 1–3
behavior: correlation-based law of effect 83–4; operant 80–2
Bernardin, H.J.; and Buckley, M.R. 49
Blessing White Inc. 136
Borman, W.C. 49, 52; and Motowidlo, S.J. 51
Boudreau, J.; and Cascio, W. 80
Bowers, C.A.; Salas, E. and Milham, L.M. 24
Bowling, N.A.; *et al* 78–9
Brief, A.P.; and Atieh, J.M. 7
Brisson, C.; *et al* 12
Buckley, F.; and Chughtai, A.A. 136
Buckley, M.R.; and Bernardin, H.J. 49
Bucklin, B.R.: Austin, J.T. and Alvero, A. 66; *et al* 86, 101–3

Cameron, J.; Eisenberger, R. and Rhoades, L. 9
Canon-Bowers, J.A.; and Salas, E. 24
Capaldi, E.J. 82
Cardy, R.L.; and Dobbins, G.H. 49
Carroll, V.; Friedman, M.D. and Rosenman, R.D. 10
Cascio, W.; and Boudreau, J. 80
Catania, A.C. 81
Chatman, J.A. 111
Chughtai, A.A.; and Buckley, F. 136

Civil Rights Act (1964) 65
Cleveland, J.N.; Murphy, K.R. and Williams, R.E. 47, 50
cognitive evaluation theory (CET) 9–10
Continental Airlines 55
Crowell, C.R. 65; *et al* 108; Hantula, D.A. and McArthur, K.L. 2–3, 100–13
customer observation questionnaire (COQ) 106–9; customer relations score 107–8, **109**; incentive 106–7; interventions 108–9; questions 109; reliability 108; return rate 106–7; verification 107; *yes* responses 109, 110

Daniels, A.C. 21, 86, 137–9; and Daniels, J.E. 138–9
Deci, E.L.; and Ryan, R.M. 9
defective parts per million (DPPM) 89
Delery, J.E.; *et al* 105
Deming, W.E. 138
DeNisi, A.S. 2, 46–57; and Kluger, A.N. 50–1
Dobbins, G.H.; and Cardy, R.L. 49
Dougherty, T.W.; and Howard, L.W. 14–15
Dunnette, M.D. 48
Dweck, C. 123; *et al* 122

Eisenberger, R.; Rhoades, L. and Cameron, J. 9
Emergency Medical Service (EMS) managers 23, 28
employee: control 7–8, 14; motivation 6; performance 2; well-being 8, 11–17
employee engagement 3, 135–40; autonomy 139; behavioral 137; emotional 136; experimental causality 139–40; job characteristics 136; rational 136; variables 136
experimental causality 139–40

Farmer, S.M.; Tierney, P. and Kung-McIntyre, K. 127
Farr, J.L.: and Jacobs, R. 112; and Landy, F.J. 48, 62, 63
Filipkowski, M.; and Johnson, C.M. 88–90
Frazier, C.B.; and Ludwig, T.D. 3, 135–40
Fredrickson, B. 120, 129

INDEX

Friedman, M.D.; Rosenman, R.D. and Carroll, V. 10

Gallup Employee Engagement Survey Analysis Tool (ESAT) 135–6
Ganster, D.C.; *et al* 2, 5–17
Geller, E.S. 137–8; and Ludwig, T.D. 139
Gentili, S.; Pede, S. and Timio, M. 11
Gravina, N.E. 138; and Siers, B.P. 2, 61–9
Green, L.; *et al* 87
Guion, R. 65

Hall, B.L. 91
Hantula, D.A.: and Kondash, J. 78; McArthur, K.L. and Crowell, C.R. 2–3, 100–13
happiness 91
Hawthorne effect/studies 101–2
Heinzmann, A.T.; Lawson, L. and Komaki, J.L. 21
Hobson's Choice 78–9, 90
Hopkins, B. 81, 86
Houlfort, N.; *et al* 9
House Leadership model 77
Howard, L.W.; and Dougherty, T.W. 14–15
Hull, C.L. 74
Hyten, C. 62

I-O Psychology (IOP) 67–9, 72, 88–91, 101, 111–13
Immerwahr, J.; and Yankelovich, D. 111
in-basket assessment 28, 42
Industrial and Organizational Psychology (IOP) 1–3, 61–2, 65; attitude measures 89; behavior 73–5; features 101–2; grand theory 74; job analysis 102; OBM 68–9, 72, 88–91, 101, 111–13; personnel selection 102; psychologists 48; satisfaction 102; studies 102; techniques 102
interrater agreement 34

Jacobs, R.; and Farr, J. 112
job satisfaction 73, 76–8, 88; and attitudes 76; definition 76; scales 76–7
Johnson, C.M.: and Beehr, T.A. 1–3; and Filipkowski, M. 88–90

Karasek, R. 14
Kluger, A.N.; and DeNisi, A.S. 50–1
Komaki, J.L. 22, 28; *et al* 2, 20–43, 52; Heinzmann, A.T. and Lawson, L. 21; and Reynard Minnich, M. 67, 86
Kondash, J.; and Hantula, D.A. 78
Kung-McIntyre, K.; Farmer, S.M. and Tierney, P. 127

Landy, F.J.; and Farr, J.L. 48, 62–3
Langton, N.; and Pfeffer, J. 8

Latham, G.P.: *et al* 64; and Mann, S. 62, 65
Lawson, L.; Komaki, J.L. and Heinzmann, A.T. 21
leadership 20–43; critical operant-based 20–43, *see also* Operant Model of Effective Supervision
Levi, L. 10–11
Lewin, K. 74, 80
line of sight problem 56
Locke, E.A. 76
Ludwig, T.D. 3, 138; and Frazier, C.B. 3, 135–40; and Geller, E.S. 139
Luthans, F. 118; Youssef, C.M. and Avolio, B.J. 119; Youssef, C.M. and Rawski, S.L. 3, 117–31

McArthur, K.L.; Crowell, C.R. and Hantula, D.A. 2–3, 100–13
Macey, W.H.; and Schneider, B. 136
MacKenzie, S.B.; Organ, D.W. and Podsakoff, P.M. 104
McMahon, M.; Wilder, D.A. and Rost, K. 86
Mager, R.F.; and Pipe, P. 21
management behaviors 138–9
managers (effective) study 23–43; assessment methods 24; categories and diferences 29–30, 34–6; control group 29, 36, 37–8, **39**, 41; course evaluation questionnaire 40–1; EMS 23, 28; examples and feedback 35; interrater agreement 34; merchandising agency 28; monitoring 40, 41–2; observations 28; participants 28–9, 42; positive consequences 30, **39**, 41; responses 24–5; scoring 30, 34; simulation and setting 27–8; training evaluation experiments 25–6; training (Operant Model based) 34–5, 40–1; treatment group 29, 36, 41; variables 26–7, *see also* Operant Model of Effective Supervision
Mann, S.; and Latham, G.P. 62, 65
mastery orientation 122–6
Mawhinney, T.C. 2, 72–91, 138
Methot, L.L.; *et al* 28
Michael, J. 81
Milham, L.M.; Bowers, C.A. and Salas, E. 24
Motivational Effectiveness Exercise (MEE) 28–34, 31–3, 37–8, 42; select categories bar chart **39**
Motowidlo, S.J.; and Borman, W.C. 51
Muller, W.M.; and Silverman, S.B. 63
Murphy, K.R.; Williams, R.E. and Cardy, R.L. 47, 50

negativity 120

operant conditioning 21
Operant Model of Effective Supervision 22–3, 34–5; antecedents 21–3, 30, 36, 40, 41–2; consequences 22; studies 22–3; tests 23; training 34–5, *see also* managers (effective) study

INDEX

Organ, D.W.; Podsakoff, P.M. and MacKenzie, S.B. 104
Organizational Behavior Management (OBM) 1–3, 48, 61–4, 81–2, 137, 140; consequences 111; critique 112; DPPM 89; features 102–3; and I-O Psychology 67–9, 72, 88–91, 101, 111–13; interventions 111; on-task behaviour 89; studies 103, 111
organizational behavior modification (OB Mod) 117–18, 118, 131
organizational citizenship behavior (OCB) 76, 104

Parsons, H. 113
Parsons, M.B. 84, 85; and Reid, D.H. 86
partial reinforcement extinction effect (PREE) 82
pay; variable plans 6
Pede, S.; Timio, M. and Gentili, S. 11
performance 90; contextual 51–2; dependent 55; direct observations 64; firm level 54–6; independent 55; individual 54–5; team 55
performance appraisals 46–57, 61–9; competency models 67; data 68; fairness 50; feedback 50–3; input 67–8; output 68; purpose 47–9; rating scales 47–50
performance management process 47, 52–3, 61, 66–9; activities 52; definition 65; functions 63; goal-setting 53; top down 56
performance-based pay 6–17; disability after retirement 12; field experiments 10–11, 16; job characteristics and type 13–15; laboratory experiments 9–11; monitoring 13; nonexperimental field studies 11–16; payment strategies 14; piecework rate *vs.* hourly wage 10–12, 16; plans 16; survey study 13; threat or challenge 7; turnover 15
Pfeffer, J. 8, 16; and Langton, N. 8
piecework 10–12, 16
Pipe, P.; and Mager, R.F. 21
Podsakoff, P.M.: MacKenzie, S.B. and Organ, D.W. 104; and Scott, W.E. 82
Porter, C. 55
positive organizational behavior (POB) study 117–31; case problems 125; coding 126; definition 119; feedback 125–6, 129; hypotheses 121–4, 127–8; implications 129; integrated positivity model 118; limitations 130; performance assessment 126–7; positive-to-negative ratio 121–2; procedure 124–5; quality and quantity 126–7; regressions 127; reported innovation 127; results 127–9, **128**; sample and survey 124–5; strengths 130
positive psychology 119–24, 135
positivity 120–4, 129–30
Pritchard, R.D.; *et al* 54
Productivity Measurement and Enhancement System (ProMES) 54
psychological capital (PsyCap) 118–30; resources 120–2
Pulakos, E.D. 49

Rawski, S.L.; Luthans, F. and Youssef, C.M. 3, 117–31
Redmon, W.K. 88; and Wilk, L.A. 87–8
Reid, D.H.; and Parsons, M.B. 86
reinforcement 83, 137–8
reward systems 5–9
Reynard Minnich, M.; and Komaki, J.L. 67, 86
Rhoades, L.; Cameron, J. and Eisenberger, R. 9
Riketta, M.R. 78
Rosenman, R.D.; Carroll, V. and Friedman, M.D. 10
Rost, K.; McMahon, M. and Wilder, D.A. 86
Ryan, R.M.; and Deci, E.L. 9

Saks, A.M. 136–7
Salas, E. 24; and Canon-Bowers, J.A. 24; Milham, L.M. and Bowers, C.A. 24
Sayles, L. 24
Schleicher, D.J.; *et al* 76–80, 89
Schneider, B.; and Macey, W.H. 136
Schwartz, I.S.; and Baer, D.M. 84–5, 91
Scott, W.E.; and Podsakoff, P.M. 82
service industry 104; value added dimension 104
service technicians (STs) 104–9; behavioral selection system 105–6; customer perceptions 106; feedback 108; job analysis 105; observer 107; questionnaire *see* customer observation questionnaire (COQ); value-added behavior 106; withdrawal stage 108
Siers, B.P.; and Gravina, N.E. 2, 61–9
Silverman, S.B.; and Muller, W.M. 63
Skinner, B.F. 74–5, 80–3, 86, 102–3, 112, 138
Smith, F.J. 79
Smith, M.J.; *et al* 13
Smith, P.C. 76, 78
Social Validity (SV) 84–5
springboards 110
stress 7; hormones 10–11; transactional model 7; workplace 5
SURF & C criteria 52

task clarification 111
Tierney, P.; Kung-McIntyre, K. and Farmer, S.M. 127
Timio, M.: and Gentili, S. 10–11; Gentili, S. and Pede, S. 11
Towers Perrin 136
training 34–5, 40–1; employee productivity/manager supervisory skills experiments 25–6

Uniform Guidelines on employee selection procedures 66

INDEX

valence, instrumentality, expectancy (V-I-E) work motivation theory 75–6, 83; motivational force (MF) 77; variations 77
Vargas, J.S. 81
Villanova, P.: and Austin, J. 112; and Austin, J.T. 64
Vroom, V.H. 74–5

Watson, J.B. 101
Weinshank, B. 28
Weitz, J. 52
Wertheimer, M. 73
Wexley, K.N. 24
Wilder, D.A.; Rost, K. and McMahon, M. 86

Wilk, L.A.; and Redmon, W.K. 87–8
Williams, K.J.; et al 47
Williams, R.E.; Cardy, R.L. and Murphy, K.R. 47, 50
Wolf, M.M. 85

Yankelovich, D.; and Immerwahr, J. 111
Youssef, C.M.: Avolio, B.J. and Luthans, F. 119; Rawski, S.L. and Luthans, F. 3, 117–31

Zedeck, S. 73–4, 76
Zemke, R.; and Albrecht, K. 104

www.routledge.com/9780415576710

Related titles from Routledge

Understanding Complexity in Organizations

Behavioral Systems

Edited by Timothy Ludwig and Ramona Houmanfar

Organizations are complex entities that must adapt the practices of their employees and management to meet the demands of a dynamic environment. They are behavioral systems that coordinate interactions among its members and environment. Changing practices in one area of an organization can generate a reaction throughout the entire system, thus affecting the behaviors of those working within other areas, the experience of customers, and important organizational results.

This book contains articles by internationally recognized experts in Behavioral Systems Analysis who discuss the role of organizational practices in their study of performance improvement and cultural change from both practical and conceptual perspectives.

This book was published as a special issue in the *Journal of Organizational Behavior Management*.

March 2010: 246 x 174: 264pp
Hb: 978-0-415-57670-1
£75 / $125

For more information and to order a copy visit
www.routledge.com/9780415576710

Available from all good bookshops

Related titles from Routledge

www.routledge.com/9780415519205

Consumer Behavior Analysis
A Rational Approach to Consumer Choice

Edited by Donald A. Hantula and Victoria K. Wells

Consumption is the primary economic activity in a post-industrial society. We are consumers, not producers. Consumer Behavior Analysis is leading heterodox marketing scholarship and innovative applied behavioral work, with much to offer both constituencies. This book shows how Consumer Behavior Analysis fits within a larger-scale approach to Marketing, Consumer Psychology, Behavior Analysis and Organizational Behavior Management. Describing both theoretical analyses as well as empirical studies including laboratory experiments in e-commerce, in-store experiments in grocery shopping, and an analysis of the counterfeit goods market, this book is a working example of translational research.

This book was originally published as a special issue of the *Journal of Organizational Behavior Management.*

February 2013: 246 x 174: 208pp
Hb: 978-0-415-51920-5
£80 / $125

For more information and to order a copy visit
www.routledge.com/9780415519205

Available from all good bookshops